In The Furtherance of Justice

Based on True Events of a DEA Agent and Two Private Investigators

I0104136

Dianne DeMille, Ph.D.
Larry Ray Hardin
Jeffrey Pearce
Randy Torgerson

Third Edition of *Path of the Devil*

Dianne DeMille PhD, Larry Hardin, Jeffrey Pearce, Randy Torgerson

February 2024
Dianne's Consultant Services
Anaheim, CA

ISBN: 979-8-9896649-2-4 Paperback
ISBN: 979-8-9896649-3-1 eBook
ISBN: 978-1-7360941-8-1 POTD Audio Book

"**A close friend** and retired DEA agent recommended this book and glad he did! The corruption in our country has been growing for decades and this book is an expose of the politicians as well as lack of cooperation at almost every level of law enforcement. Thanks to the commitment of dedicated agents and PI's who are honest and moral to share their investigation with all of us! Good vs Evil is putting it mildly!" Michael Kelly, Television Producer/Director

Feared for their lives: "It contained some harrowing moments where investigators feared for their lives and had to think quickly to save themselves, sometimes lying their way out of trouble. This gave a great feel for the seriousness of the situation, how far the investigators would go, and how far the cartels went to hide their activities from the law." Kirkus Review

Corruption of our protectors! "I bought this eBook after listening to the True Crime Tuesday podcast with Larry. I am upset and shocked to learn the corruption within DEA, law enforcement and the judicial system dealing with drug enforcement. If it this bad with these agencies, the corruption in local, state and federal government agencies must be worse than I imagined. It was a little hard to read, for me, with all the names and jumping around to the different people's stories, but I did understand the book. The honesty of Larry is to be honored. May peace be with him and is family." *Roland Alwin Kuhleman*

Great Read: "Great book. Shows what the first line of defense for what an American citizen has to do to try and protect our way of life. Sad commentary on the illegal and immoral things some people in our government do to thwart the hard work done by our law enforcement." *Ray*

Easy Read: "This was an interesting book, easy to read as it took you through the dangers of drugs and the investigations. I took away from the book to not trust our government and as a citizen we should do everything we can to stop using drugs, stop our children from using because only a few really care. Money controls the border,

Dianne DeMille PhD, Larry Hardin, Jeffrey Pearce, Randy Torgerson

Drugs control the border, and the users are victims. Supply and Demand." *Sindi McGuire*

Entertaining stories: "The format is interesting - the stories are told by the different authors and they each have their own viewpoints to share. You will find yourself going through page-turning mode, for sure!" *J.J.*

Fast Paced: "the novel is fast-paced and written in a way that keeps the reader wondering what will happen next." Kirkus Review

A Mind opening account into the world of illicit drugs: "The Book focuses on a specific drug cartel and their activities and leaves you wanting the good guys to win! If you are a theorist, it will bring you to give pause why Path of the Devil reveals why things happen and do not happen and the corruption that lies within." *Carol Mosser*

A Powerful Story: "A powerful story filled with money, murder, corruption, and deceit. … Gave a great feel for the seriousness of the situation, how far the investigators would go, and how far the cartels went to hide their activities from the law." *Onlinbookclulb.com*

"Have you ever wondered why we can't win the war on drugs?" *unamilagra*

You have to read this book! "Awesome Book, really felt like I was in the story, watching from the bleachers, what a great job everyone did to make it come alive. Will defiantly recommend it to anyone who wants to dive into a crime fighting realistic read!!" *Bruce Rustman*

Interesting Read: "Had good detail and humor mixed together, makes for a good quick read you can't put down!" *Barry Legend*

Great Book: "Once I started to read this book. I could not put it down and finished it a short time. One of the best books I have read in a while." *Mark Becker*

Arduous Investigation: "An often-engrossing glimpse into an arduous criminal investigation, despite some missteps." Kirkus Review

In Memory of

Jeffrey Pearce & Jerry Pearce

Jeffrey Pearce was our friend and companion both during the Path of the Devil investigation and for all the years after. He was a courageous and unique man. He was honest to a fault by telling it as he saw it. Jeff worked hard all his life and there was much more to him than this one case in this book. Jeff was inspirational and forced those around him to be better than they were. We lost Jeff on August 24, 2020, from Covid-19 and underlying health conditions. We miss him and love him. Our prayers go to his family and friends. Stay safe my brother, my friend. You are at peace.

Jerry Pearce was Jeff and Randy's boss and mentor. He was Larry's friend and confidant. He was generous, a loving husband, and a hardcore leader. Jerry taught everyone around him many life lessons. He looked out for those who counted on him. He was stubborn at times, but he knew how to run his business. Because of Jerry's connections in getting this case, we learned lessons that could otherwise never be taught. Jerry's heart was huge even if you didn't always see it right away. Jerry left us January 8, 2018, due to natural causes. Stay safe my mentor, my friend. You are at peace.

Dianne DeMille PhD, Larry Hardin, Jeffrey Pearce, Randy Torgerson

Foreword

Growing up in the South Bronx, my father once told me: "True hell is being the only guy playing straight in a dirty card game." He was talking about Street fighting, but he might just as well have been talking about my 25-year career as a DEA undercover agent. The undercovers went after their targets like hungry wolves, crossing borders with false identities into dark parts of the world where our targets had the power of life and death that only God or the devil should have. This reality only made us hungrier to bring them down; to destroy them. It felt like God's work. So, we threw ourselves into these missions with the total abandon of our safety and our families, with the abiding belief that, at the very least, our missions and goals were supported by the full might of the United States government. Too many of us, like DEA agent, Enrique Kiki Camarena, tortured to a grotesque death by Mexican police and drug traffickers, would die, because of that false belief. A few of us, like myself, defied those black odds and lived to tell the story of the dirtiest card game in American history– the war on drugs. And now comes, my colleagues, Larry Ray Hardin and his partners Jeffrey Pearce and Randy Torgerson with their aptly titled, nonfiction expose "Path of the Devil," to remind America, that this dirty and deadly game is still very much alive and well.

—Michael Levine, NY Times bestselling author of "Deep Cover" and "The Big White Lie."

Dianne DeMille PhD, Larry Hardin, Jeffrey Pearce, Randy Torgerson

Author's Note

The story you are about to read is based on true events. Names of individuals and businesses have been changed for protection. Incidents, events, and conversations have been created by the authors.

Dianne DeMille PhD, Larry Hardin, Jeffrey Pearce, Randy Torgerson

Introduction

This story is based on true events of three men determined to bring down a notorious drug cartel operating along the southwestern border of the United States. For five years the men spearheaded separate but simultaneous investigations in different locations around the country. According to a March 1997 report by Mike Gallegher, investigative reporter for the Albuquerque Journal, along the border between United States and Mexico, from Tijuana, Mexico/San Diego, California to Matamoros, Mexico/Brownsville, Florida, there are twelve Gatekeepers who form "a syndicate of the major drug cartels operating in Mexico."[1] The syndicate controls specific regions for smuggling narcotics and drugs into the U.S. and transportation of weapons to Central and South America. The cartels "coordinate bribes at the national level, oversee money laundering operations and negotiate the shipment of drugs at the international level."[2]

One case, conducted by DEA Agent Larry Ray Hardin, took place in Yuma and San Luis, both cities in Arizona. Another case occurred simultaneously in Los Angeles, California, and was conducted by private investigators Jeff Pearce and Randy Torgerson of the Pearce Corporation. About one year into the cases, they found themselves making connections with the Meraz organization, a drug cartel in San Luis, Rio Colorado, Mexico, and their associations and businesses conducted in Los Angeles.

Experiences from their investigation, surveillance, and collection of intelligence to build the cases present a compelling story leading to what became of the Meraz family, their organization, and the three young men. The intensity of this work – and in some instances, the fun times – relate how events such as these shaped each of their lives.

Dianne DeMille PhD, Larry Hardin, Jeffrey Pearce, Randy Torgerson

In The Furtherance of Justice

Table of Contents

In The Furtherance of Justice

Prologue

1975

In 1975, DEA agents Don Ware and Roy Stevenson were in the thick of a Mexican heroin investigation. They'd been making progress when things took a turn for the worse, as they often do in drug-related situations. The cartel had targeted them for murder.

The two agents focused on the Meraz brothers, a cartel known as much for the excessive amount of drugs they sold, as their coldhearted killing. Don and Roy's confidential informant (CI) was poised to make a buy from one of the brothers. Don, Roy, and the rest of their team were prepared and anticipating anything that might go wrong, which often did in the world of drug trafficking. Fellow DEA agents set up surveillance in the center of the desert town to watch their CI make a heroin deal, and Don and Roy were ready to make a big bust.

They jumped in their '74 Chevy pickup truck and took off for the northern part of town to observe the deal. Minutes into their journey, they realized they were being followed by a black and red car and it was racing toward them. It accelerated ahead then cut them off. Although highly experienced and well trained, their hearts raced uncontrollably. They knew they were in serious trouble.

The occupants exited their car and pointed guns at Don and Roy. Another car full of Mexicans pulled up in front of them and the gunmen forced the agents out of the truck. Don and Roy had no choice but to comply. Wordlessly, they left the safety of their truck. The Mexicans wasted no time getting to work and sending a message, beating them with their guns, pistol whipping them in the face and slamming their weapons into the sides of their heads, until both men were incapacitated. Once on the ground, they were stomped and kicked until the agents were severely injured.

They lifted the injured agents, tossing them into the open bed of Don's pickup. One of the Mexicans jumped into the driver's side of the truck and sped away with the agents lying helplessly in the back.

Roy and Don knew they were about to die. Ron said, "We have to do something, or we're going to end up in the desert." They both knew what that meant. You don't come back from the desert. Don was critically injured but able to tell Roy, "Don't worry, my little snub-nose fell down to my crotch." His captors had failed to search Don below the waistband. Many law enforcement agents carry their gun in their pants because attackers will avoid touching the crotch area.

Don couldn't reach the .38 caliber; he was too broken. Roy was injured too, but able to move around some. They raised themselves up to see where they were headed and discuss how they might escape. They noticed a car following close behind with two other men watching them.

The truck had only gone about a block when Don noticed a bus ahead of them. He said to Roy, "Get my gun, and as soon as the truck stops, I want you to end this. Make the driver stop, and then we're both getting out." They didn't have much to work with, and the men in the car following had eyes on them. Their options were few, but their instincts were sharp. Although they knew there was a good chance, they wouldn't make it out alive, if there were any chance in hell of making it, they were going for it.

When the pickup stopped, Roy was able to climb out with the gun. He walked up to the driver and pointed it directly into his face. Since Roy spoke Spanish fluently, he was able to tell the driver to let them go. The driver tried to punch him. Roy had neither the time or inclination to fight, so he shot him in the face. The man collapsed onto the steering wheel.

Roy planned to return to the truck and lift Don from the back but saw his partner had already rolled out and was running to the side of the road. Don didn't look like he knew what he was doing or where he was going. Ron caught up to him quickly and grabbed him by the arm. He was going to take him to an old car junkyard on

2

the side of the road to wait for backup. The two Mexicans who had been watching from the car got out and started shooting. Both agents took several hits.

The men lay bleeding in the middle of the road. When the shooters ran out of bullets, Roy pretended to be dead and told Don to do the same. The strategy worked, and the shooters disappeared from the scene moments later in their own vehicles.

Don was shot four times. As he lay face down in the street, he thought his life was over. People walked by, but no one would stop. He asked for a priest. But the citizens of the city knew better than to help a gringo who'd been messing with the cartel.

Roy was shot once in the leg and once in the back. He pulled himself up and hobbled to his truck. He was able to get to the radio and call for help. He put the car in drive but almost hit his partner before realizing his right leg wasn't working right.

Help arrived before long, and Roy was taken to a hospital in Yuma. Don was in worse shape. It was feared he wouldn't make the drive and was taken to the hospital in Mexico, which was closer.

Don was lucky to survive but suffered from pain for many years. He died in 2004 in surgery due to complications from his injuries.

The Mexican Federal Attorney in San Luis, Mexico initiated federal arrest warrants against the Meraz brothers – Olegario, Oswaldo, and Oscar Meraz-Gutierrez – and their associates for involvement in the attempted murder of Don Ware and Roy Stevenson.

Oswaldo and his brothers, Olegario and Oscar, were arrested in San Luis in 1975. Later, the Mexican Federal Judicial charged Olegario for being responsible for the kidnapping and shooting.[3] Oscar told a Mexican police officer, "I'm unhappy that the DEA agents were not killed in San Luis. We intended to murder them."

Dianne DeMille PhD, Larry Hardin, Jeffrey Pearce, Randy Torgerson

Chapter 1: New to DEA; San Diego, CA

1988, Larry

I joined the San Diego DEA Office, and once I started, realized I was given a lot of power to arrest people for committing crimes. I worked primarily with narcotics but could arrest anyone for just about anything – drugs, bank robbery, or whatever. It was a little intimidating because the power and authority I had were so broad.

I became a Special Agent with the Organized Crime Drug Enforcement Task Force (OCDETF) in the San Diego DEA Office, 1988. I started working with the OCDETF narcotics street team in San Diego.

After a week on the job, my supervisor told me, "Don't get caught drinking in your government car or screwing women, especially informants." He talked about nothing else, only women and drinking.

I watched a few agents who took advantage of their position with women. I refused to participate in sex with the women on the streets or the women I worked with, but I was willing to join in the drinking.

I remember once I was drinking with other agents in a bar before going home. A well-dressed young woman sat next to me. One of the agents whispered something in her ear. I figured he must know her. Suddenly she pulled up her dress with no panties on and showed her "snatch." I said out loud, "Is she crazy?" I quickly moved away from her while the other agents laughed. The temptation wasn't there for me. I stayed away from it and thanked my wife for being there for me when I got home.

I believed that once an agent got involved with sex, drugs, and dirty money, he crossed over to the dark side of corruption. Self-control was the only way around it. It was always available to anyone who wanted to take advantage of it.

For me, I stood for character, integrity, faith, loyalty, honesty, truth, and family. Most of the agents I worked with shared my values. And most of the DEA agents I worked with had the same upstanding character as well. While serving in the military, I learned people are different all over the United States and the world with varying levels of integrity.

When I talk about the dark side of my work, I'm referring to the few agents I knew who were involved in sexual misconduct, drugs, and corruption.

Later, I once stopped by the bar after working on the streets. I was driving home drunk and almost hit a car with children inside. That was the last time I drove home drunk. I considered myself very lucky.

Another time when I was working with the Narcotics Task Force (NTF), I saw one of the agents take custody of money and drugs from a Border Patrol agent at a United States Border Checkpoint in Temecula, California. The NTF agent didn't want me to count the money. I thought that if he would take money, what else would he do? I didn't want any part of working with him alone.

After a few days, a border patrol agent from the Temecula checkpoint called me and said, "That NTF Agent took $75,000 from the criminals. We took custody of twice that amount." I knew what he was getting at.

Before the agent could go on, I stopped him and said, "Don't say anything to me about money. My partner took it, I didn't take any, so you talk to him!" I wanted to make it clear I wasn't getting mixed up in any corruption.

Later that year on Thanksgiving Day, the same agent called me, "Larry, I need your help, this guy is picking up some money."

He wanted me to come with him.

Why me again?

I went with the agent to the location. After spotting the criminal in his car, the other NTF agent contacted a local police department to help stop the car for a traffic violation. I observed an officer driving a marked unit stop the guy's car. When the guy got out, I approached him with my handgun pointed at his chest. "Open the trunk," I yelled.

Without hesitation, he opened the trunk.

Wow, there's a big pile of money dumped in this trunk.

I asked the driver of the car, "How much money do you think you have here?"

He told me, "About $245,000."

My partner said to me, "You go ahead and take the prisoner back to the police department, and I'll take the car back and count the money."

The next day when the story came out in the newspaper, it said the car was seized with $37,000 in it. Something wasn't right about the amount, but I didn't say anything about it to my boss. I learned quickly after one year on the job; you don't question or say anything to your boss about your senior partner's integrity.

Over the years, I heard from informants that some agents took money on the streets and other agents were criminals themselves. That was disappointing to hear, but I did work with some great agents for over 23 years.

I didn't know that was the norm. Not for all agents, but there were some. It was hard to ignore the stealing. It shook my belief in working with some agents. On one occasion, while at lunch, an NTF officer picked up two married law clerks. As I sat in the driver's seat talking with one of the girls, the officer was trying to have sex with the other girl in the backseat. As much as I wanted to tune it out, I couldn't help but hear. After dropping the girls off at the courthouse, I asked the officer, "How can you crawl in the backseat with a married woman and have sex? You have a wife and two little boys." The officer just laughed it off and asked why I didn't try to have sex with the other girl. I was appalled with his behavior, but he didn't care what I thought.

We all have faults, and I saw a lot of crazy stuff in NTF. It was up to me to say "no." A few NTF guys got drunk at work, and

I heard about the corruption of drugs and money but didn't see it, myself.

◇◇◇

In 1990, my wife was offered a job with the Department of Defense in Yuma, Arizona. I decided to put in for a transfer to Yuma as well. We had lived there a few years before. It was a small community, easy to get around, go to school, and we thought it was a great place to live. I was ready to relax a little and told my wife that when we got to Yuma, I could stop working with narcotics in San Diego. She went to Yuma, and I followed about six months later in the fall.

Also in 1990, as it turned out, Yuma was not a great place to work. It was even worse for an agent's career because you could be stuck there for years. That's a long time to spend in the turbulent, wild, west of Southern Arizona near the border of Mexico. After several months, I was ready to leave Yuma. The work was getting too demanding, and I heard from other agents about the corruption in the law enforcement community. I asked to be transferred to Puerto Rico. My request was denied.

Chapter 2: Larry Moves to Yuma, AZ

1990-1991

Yuma was a small desert town just ten miles north of the Mexican border. When I arrived, the office had four agents, a supervisor, and a secretary. Usually, there were only two agents in the office at any given time. My job at the Arizona/Mexico border was to find how drugs were entering into the U.S. through the border at San Luis, Mexico. Our DEA office took care of all the checkpoints and Ports of Entry surrounding Yuma.

Yuma was hot and humid with an average temperature of 117 F° in the summer. After a day of working on the desert mountain near the Mexican border, I'd be wet and sticky from the heat and humidity. All I wanted was to get home and hop in the shower. I'd have to peel the clothes off my body before washing the sand from my day.

Larry R Hardin 1990
539 lbs. Cocaine

We had a safe house to use as our base for all-night surveillance. About a month after arriving in Yuma, I was at the safe house playing poker with three cops working on an OCDETF case. One was in the kitchen making hot dogs and spicy Mexican chili. Several other agents and law enforcement officers were lying around on the couches and floor waiting to hear that a vehicle loaded with drugs might be traveling from a target residence in Yuma or entering the country from the Mexican border.

One of the poker players mentioned Olegario and Oscar, of the Meraz family. He explained to me, as a new agent to Yuma, that nothing comes across the Port of Entry (POE) into the U.S. from Mexico that wasn't arranged by the Meraz's. That night we got a call that one of the Meraz traffickers was moving drugs. Some of the agents took off to investigate, but I kept playing poker. I wanted to stick around and hear more stories about the Meraz brothers.

There were so many narcotics cases in Yuma County; the Meraz's had never crossed my mind. But days later, I began looking for everything I could find with the name Meraz and asked a lot of questions. I made notes from what I heard from my Sources of Information (SOI) and interviews with cops who targeted the Meraz organization for dope trafficking and other crimes. Everything started coming together. It was all there –marijuana, cocaine, heroin, corruption, and money laundering coming into the states. It seemed like every time someone in law enforcement got close to the Meraz family, and the case would be shut down before federal and state prosecutions were finalized. This family had connections like tentacles of an octopus, reaching out and grabbing people in the community. They appeared to be untouchable. But I had a sense of what I needed to do to get them prosecuted.

Going back to the 1970s, strenuous efforts by Orozco Oseguera, his brothers, his brother-in-law, and the Meraz patriarch, Olegario Meraz Gutierrez, covered up the ambush of the two DEA agents, Don and Roy. They were kidnapped, beaten, shot, and left for dead in San Luis Rio Colorado near the home of the Meraz's because they had traced the major drug operations in San Luis to the brothers.[4]

Living in Yuma, I discovered a lot about the Meraz brothers, their family, how they were entrenched in the community, and their strong family ties at the San Luis POE checkpoint. I continued hearing rumors from other DEAs, customs agents, and local Police Department (PD) and thought, *Wow, I'm going to take a look into this. Why doesn't anyone want to work on this anymore?* Thinking about their involvement in the shooting of Don and Roy as well as the kidnapping, torture, and murder of DEA Agent, Enrique (Kiki) Camarena made me even more determined.[5]

<><><>

Kiki Camarena was murdered February 9, 1985, in Mexico. Camarena was born in Mexico and became a U.S. citizen at a young age. He was a highly decorated Marine, a Vietnam vet, and a DEA agent working and living in Guadalajara with his wife and three children. "Kiki started hitting big people hard and they couldn't understand where he was getting his intel,"[6] recalled former DEA agent and Camarena friend, Tony Ayala. "He brought a lot of attention to himself"[7] and was murdered at the age of 37.[8]

Kiki had discovered a large marijuana field, approximately 2,500 acres,[9] on property owned by the Quintero cartel. The Quintero's cartel used Miguel Angel Felix-Gallardo criminal organization to move the marijuana from the southwest Mexican border into California. The cartel wanted to know what the U.S. government knew. When Mexican law enforcement wouldn't help locate Kiki, the U.S. temporarily closed the border. That's the only time in U.S. history that's happened.[10]

Kiki and his CI were kidnapped in Guadalajara. The CI was killed immediately. Kiki was not as fortunate. He was skinned alive. The cartel made an audio tape of the vicious murder. DEA agents heard Kiki screaming and crying before dying in horrible pain. A cartel doctor gave him drugs to keep him alive so they could torture him even longer.[11] DEA discovered from informants that a close relative, a woman named Magdalena Santillan Meraz, was on hand for the torture and recorded the whole thing. DEA agents later recovered the tape, and it proved to be a valuable piece of evidence.

It was the Raphael Quintero organization who kidnapped and tortured Camarena. The Meraz organization is part of that group. Alvino Quintero Meraz, a cousin to Raphael Quintero, was also arrested in the case. He was a shrimp importer in Mexicali and used the San Luis Port of Entry. Oswaldo Meraz took over Raphael's shrimp business after the death of Camarena.

Hector Berrellez was a former DEA supervisor and was awarded the prestigious DEA Administrator's Award for his work in handling and solving Camarena case.[12] He said, "Twenty-seven years ago, the kidnap, torture, and murder of a U.S. Drug Enforcement Administration agent by Mexican drug traffickers sparked one of the biggest manhunts the United States government has ever launched in North America. It also offered an ominous warning of things to come."[13]

Many of those who were involved in the kidnapping and torture were brought to trial, and three men were convicted.[14] None of those were from the Meraz organization. However, they were connected to the Meraz's.[15]

Through telephone records from January 1986, agents discovered that two of the murder defendants had made calls to Olegario Meraz at his home in San Luis. Raphael Caro Quintero, head of one of the gatekeepers, and the most powerful drug cartel in Guadalajara was sentenced to 40 years in prison according to *Huffington Post*[16] (30 years according to *LA Times*[17]). Others were also arrested. According to Chris Kaul in the *Los Angeles Times* and Luis Merentez of the *Huffington Post*, we would later learn the case was also connected to the Iran Contra scandal. Quintero was released after serving only 28 years because of a technicality.[18, 19]

Although agents continuously tried to penetrate their group, they consistently failed. The Meraz family had strong ties in the law enforcement community and were very active in Yuma and San Luis, Arizona. They operated with impunity for more than 20 years. From what I could tell, the Yuma law enforcement community at the Port of Entry was tragically corrupt.

With Don and Roy always in mind, I pushed myself to focus on the Meraz brothers. I'd never met either of them, but they were part of my DEA family, and this drove my determination to arrest the Meraz's. Even though I was working some other good criminal cases at the same time. I was going to go after the brothers – slowly and cautiously. I needed to be careful and keep it very quiet within my office. Even though I worked with both good and bad cops, I never forgot I had to be cautious. It was a small town, and I wasn't sure who I could trust in law enforcement. I truly felt like I was on my own.

<><><>

I opened a case on the Meraz's drug activities and was finding information from a variety of sources. I discovered years of phone records from the hitmen behind the attempted murder of Don and Roy calling the Olegario Meraz home.[20] Other calls were going into the Meraz homes in 1985 during the time Kiki Camarena and his CI were tortured and killed.

<><><>

I often did surveillance of the border at San Luis from the Rocky Mountains overlooking the town of Yuma. When I went to Mexico with one of the border patrol agents, and we returned to Yuma from the POE, I looked toward the mountains on the east side of Yuma. I once asked a border patrol agent, "How far do those mountains over there go down to Mexico from Arizona?"

"That mountain range runs from the Sonora Mexico region up to Yuma County," he said. "Franciscan missionaries named the mountain range the El Camino del Diablo Rocky Mountains. They used the base of the mountain range to guide them from Mexico to Arizona and then on to California. Travelers talked about the trail being more deadly than going through Death Valley in the eighteenth century. There are many unmarked graves along the path." I thought the Meraz case was like the El Camino Del Diablo. I decided to name it "Camino del Diablo." Path of the Devil.

<><><>

There were so many narcotics cases coming out of Mexico that we stayed busy. I would often cross the border to San Luis, Sonora, Mexico, and I spent more time there than Yuma. I could travel alone across the border into Mexico without anyone stopping me. Sometimes I drank beer while following the criminals into pool halls and bars.

Beer and food were cheap across the border. I drank a few beers and ate a grilled chicken as I watched drug trafficking locations. The criminals knew I was down there. When I returned to the U.S. at the POE checkpoint, customs and immigration wanted to know my purpose in Mexico. I would tell them I went fishing or did a little work, whatever. Without showing my badge, they knew I was a DEA agent. I had that kind of recognized authority.

I never had any problems until I started to focus on the Meraz brothers and their illegal activities.

I didn't want to deal with U.S. Customs Inspectors at the POE. According to my sources, there were some corrupt customs agents and INS officers working at the checkpoint. I didn't want anyone suspecting I was in Mexico looking into the Meraz brother's activities.

One time I took a shortcut around the border checkpoint through the open desert. When I crossed into the U.S., several customs agents and immigration officers followed me. I stopped my car. They immediately drew their guns on me, and I showed my DEA badge. They asked me to return to the POE office. When I went back to the POE, they questioned me about my failure to enter correctly. I told them, "You've got some corrupt guys working here. I didn't want to identify myself to the wrong guy at the gate."

But that was the old days. Later, I found out customs and INS had written I was a "border jumper" in their reports because I crossed the border without telling anyone who I was.

<>><>

After I was entrenched in the DEA Yuma office, the office increased personnel numbers up to four agents. Usually, there were only two agents in the office at one time. My partner was Norman, and sometimes, I worked closely with Jorge.

Later, we hired a student aide, a young 16-year-old girl, to help with the paperwork. Within a few months after hiring her, the secretary told me one of our married agents was "rubbing her breast in the file room." That same day, I told the agent, "Be careful what you do in the office with the girl." He just laughed.

A few days later, the secretary told me again, "The aide is having a relationship with that agent."

I told her, "I'll talk to the agent."

She said, "If you don't tell the agent to stop, the girl is going to lose her job."

After working for about 12 hours one night, I decided to go home. It was late in the evening, and I told the agent, "Lock up the office and turn on the security alarm when you leave."

I left the agent with the student aide in the office alone. I was so tired it didn't occur to me what could happen if I left them alone.

I went out the front door. Then I realized I had to return to pick up some paperwork. I decided to enter through the back door of the file room. As I came into the office, I saw the agent with his pants down around his ankles, positioned between the girl's legs. Her big breasts were almost exposed, and the agent was trying to suck them.

I yelled, emphatically at both, "Knock that shit off!"

The girl looked at me and ran into the supervisor's office. The agent didn't get to finish the job but had a smile on his face as he tried to pull up his pants.

I walked by the agent and over to my desk, picked up the papers I needed, turned, and walked out of the office. The agent followed me, still trying to pull up his pants. He was laughing and said to me, "I screwed her on the boss's desk the other day."

Don't do that in the office anymore!"

Shortly after, the student aide quit working for us.

There's nothing new about agents screwing a coworker, attorney, law clerk, informant, married woman, churchgoing woman, or prostitute. It was part of the job for a few of them. I couldn't understand how they loved their wives and children yet screwed any woman that dropped her panties.

<><><>

My partner, Norman, received a call from the Mexican prosecutor in San Luis, Sonora. The prosecutor had some information about Don and Roy's suspects. Later that day, we met with the Mexican prosecutor, and I asked him about the Meraz brothers. He told me, "I'm working on several other ongoing cases involving the Meraz family."

He didn't mention the Meraz's again. But he showed me boxes of investigative reports written by FBI, DEA, customs, etc.

I was shocked to see nothing redacted on the reports like agent names, case-related file numbers, or informant numbers. The prosecutor let me continue to review the reports in the boxes. There were names of other agents involved in ongoing investigative cases and the method of how the Mexican defendants were trafficking their drugs. I even saw the CI numbers on the reports.

I asked the Mexican prosecutor for the boxes, and he told me, "They belong to someone else."

I asked him, "How did you get them?"

"I received them from the U.S. Attorney's office when I was checking on cases related to Mexicans arrested in the U.S. It's called discovery. The cartels use it to learn how DEA operates in the states."

I was thinking to myself: It's incredible that DEA can't win the war on drugs. The criminals are always one step ahead of us.

Once we returned to Yuma, I reported what I saw at the Mexican prosecutor's office to my boss and DEA legal counsel in Washington, D.C.

<><><>

Sources later informed me that Olegario Meraz had been a partner to Ralph Guzman in the produce business in the San Luis area for many years. Ralph owned a produce outlet, less than 100 yards from San Luis, Mexico at the border. DEA seized properties in the area from other Meraz associates because of their involvement with narcotics trafficking.[21] I later asked Ralph if he was the United States contact for Olegario Meraz's narcotic activities. He denied any involvement but admitted he was aware of Olegario's drug operations.

I was convinced that both U.S. and Mexican officials were corrupt. Sources provided information that confirmed it. The Meraz's confirmed it. They bragged to sources that the U.S. furnished protection and cooperation with the Meraz brothers.

I was facing a complicated problem. I was the primary agent in this case, and because of the corruption, working without support. At first, I trusted those in my office, but one agent would go out and talk to other law enforcement agents about me behind my back about how I was working on the Meraz investigation with private investigators.

Through my sources, I established that the alleged corrupt officials were, most likely, the overriding factor in the Meraz trafficking success in Mexico and the U.S.

<><><>

It was early 1991 and Don Ware, who was left for dead in 1975, was living in Las Vegas and still working for the DEA. He was in constant pain and had been through several surgeries. I didn't get the opportunity to meet with Don, personally, but I knew he could provide a lot of information about the Meraz involvement in the kidnapping.

I called Don and introduced myself. "I'm going to get those Meraz brothers for what they tried to do to you and Roy."

Don told me, "That would be great!" He filled me in on the details of what went down in San Luis. Some of what I learned from him was never in the reports I'd read. There was no one I could trust without risking the Meraz's finding out. *I didn't want some corrupt cop knowing that I spoke with Don.*

<><><>

I went to the Assistant United States Attorney (AUSA), Michael Hope in Phoenix. I presented him with what I knew so far about the Meraz brothers, and he was encouraging. He told me, "Let's go ahead and open up an investigation."

Michael knew the Meraz's were behind the attempted murder of the agents in 1975, and there were U.S. warrants for their arrest and search warrants from the Mexican authorities. And somehow, the Meraz brothers were never arrested.

Michael told me, "We need to pursue this again!"

Like me, AUSA Hope was upset with the corruption of law enforcement and advised me to be careful with the investigation. He knew the border was a hazardous place. I told him I was more worried about United States Customs and Immigration Officers than agents on the Mexican border. AUSA Hope mentioned the Meraz case to Janet Napolitano, United States Attorney for Arizona.

In March 1991, after meeting with AUSA Hope, I initiated an elaborate conspiracy using my informants to target Oswaldo's shrimp business in Mexico. It was difficult to find an informant who wasn't Mexican and had a shrimp business. Since I knew from past investigations that one of the brothers had a problem with drugs and a weakness for young girls, I found my weak link and a way into the Meraz family. While the informants were meeting with Oswaldo in San Luis, I continued to learn about the family oriented Meraz organization. Sources told me they were using underground tunnels to transport large quantities of heroin, cocaine, and marijuana from San Luis, Mexico into San Luis, Arizona. Outside the tunnel, they were primarily dealing cocaine and heroin that were cost-effective for concealing and transporting in large quantities via produce and shrimp. Heroin was secondary to cocaine because it wasn't always available. Although marijuana was profitable and plentiful, it required additional manpower and more effort to conceal, smuggle, and transport.

<><><>

That summer, along with United States Customs, I asked the Department of Defense (DoD) Geophysical Survey Team to help locate this possible underground tunnel near the San Luis Port-of-Entry. DoD personnel revealed there was a 95% chance that an underground tunnel did indeed exist.

The Organized Crime Drug Enforcement Task Forces (OCDETF) had been developed in 1982 to create "a comprehensive attack against organized drug traffickers"[22] and money laundering. DEA agents ran the local OCDETF, and all members became Deputy Sheriffs with credentials to arrest people on federal or state charges.

With the approval of the AUSA office in Phoenix, I was able to build a specialized law enforcement local group in Yuma to work with me to focus solely on the Meraz investigation. The OCDETF were from local offices of DEA, United States Customs, United States Attorney's Office, Yuma County Sherriff's Department, Yuma Police Department, San Luis Police Department, and several other law enforcement agencies in the area.[23]

Our investigation was unique because it incorporated the Meraz trafficking organization with Colombia, Mexico, Southeast Asia, and the United States into a conspiracy to smuggle large quantities of narcotics into the United States and launder vast amounts of U.S. currency to Mexico and Colombia.

The Meraz's were tied to arms smuggled down to Nicaragua through Mexico and weapons traded for narcotics. I was stationed in Yuma for three-and-a-half years and left in 1996. I heard about weapons and narcotics trades. It had been happening long before I arrived.

Corruption created many roadblocks for me. Most government agents stayed away from me because they knew to avoid corruption I needed to work alone. I only communicated with the AUSA office in Phoenix and the DEA legal department in Washington, D.C. When I needed cooperation from other agents and officers from my office or the AUSA, I wouldn't take "no" for an answer. There were some agents and cops I could count on and trust. But the only one in my office was our secretary. She kept me squared away with my paperwork and made sure everything I wrote was complete and read smoothly for the AUSA. She watched over me and protected me from the gossip in the office about why I worked alone. At that time, the only PIs I trusted were Jeff and John.

Other agents focused on their cases and careers. They wanted to become DEA supervisors or to move up in the organization. I wasn't thinking that way. Sure, I was ambitious, but it wasn't something I chose to focus on. I never thought about the paycheck, or how much money I was getting.

All I knew was that I had a job to do for Don and Roy. The Yuma DEA supervisor pushed me to move on to the next case as I completed other cases, but I wasn't going to give up until I'd charged the brothers for the attempted murder of Don and Roy.

Chapter 3: Other Drug and Corruption Cases

1989-1997, Dianne

There were several cases with the Meraz brothers that Larry and the private investigators could connect to their cases.

The Mexican cartels are known as the "greatest criminal drug threat"[24] facing America. According to Edwin Mora of Breitbart[25] 224 drug tunnels were discovered along the border between the United States and Mexico since 1990. As part of the Sinaloa drug cartel, El Chapo's first tunnel, built from Agua Prieta, Mexico, to Douglas, Arizona was 30-feet underground, four-feet wide, five-feet high, and about the length of a football field. It had a complete hydraulic system to raise the floor and reveal a ladder into the tunnel at both ends. This one was discovered in 1990 and was used by El Chapo for his second escape from prison. It has become known as "Cocaine Alley" for smuggling drugs into U.S.[26, 27, 28][29] and was found to be connected to the Meraz's.

In 1997, reports showed guerrillas of the Popular Revolutionary Army in Mexico getting weapons from drug cartels in exchange for heroin. They supplied poppy farmers with firearms to protect their poppy fields.[30] United States authorities have uncovered and destroyed 224 tunnels used to smuggle bulk quantities of illicit drugs along the United States-Mexico border since 1990.[31] Tunnels were leading from Mexico to stash houses in the U.S. near the border and into private homes or warehouses. Tunnels for cartels transporting illegal drugs are becoming very sophisticated and continue to threaten United States-Mexico border security.[32]

<><><>

Sylmar, CA

Randy Torgerson discovered telephone records and other details tied to the Meraz Organization in case documents filed at the Los Angeles Courthouse. One of the cases was in Sylmar,

California, in 1989[33], where Authorities seized 20 tons of cocaine. This was the largest drug bust to date. The operation transported 77 tons of cocaine over t Seth Mydans. "Agents Seize 20 Tons of Cocaine in Raid on Los Angeles Warehouse." The New York Times. September 30, 1989. http://www.nytimes.com/1989-09-30/us/agents-seize-20-tons-of-cocaine-in-raid-on-los-angeles-warehouse.html?pagewanted=print.hree months before the raid. At that time, 20 tons of cocaine was considered a one-week supply for Los Angeles.[34]

They arrested one of the mules, who said he was doing it because the U.S. customs agent, a relative of the Meraz brothers worked at the POE in Calexico, was letting the trucks go through.

<><><>

Guadalajara, Mexico

On May 24, 1993, Cardinal Juan Posadas Ocampo, his driver, and five innocent by-standers were shot to death from cartel assassins in Guadalajara, Mexico. Ocampo and his driver were sitting in their car at the airport. The murder of Cardinal Ocampo was one of many violent attacks by drug traffickers during increasing turf wars between smuggling groups along the Southwest U.S. and Mexican border Port of Entries.[35]

The next day, Larry's Confidential Informants (CIs) overheard the Meraz brothers talking about the Cardinal's death at their house (White House), in San Luis, Sonora, Mexico. They told the CIs about the killing of Cardinal Ocampo and that he knew there was a lot of political corruption in Baja California, Mexico with the governor's office. The Meraz brothers were joking when they said Cardinal Ocampo heard too many confessions from the dopers. DEA and FBI agents had learned quickly from Mexican informants about the assassination.

<><><>

San Luis, AZ & San Luiz, Mexico
Larry

Why does the Meraz case keep disappearing from prosecution? How is this happening? Agents or someone in local law enforcement should have put the Meraz brothers away long ago. Corruption in law enforcement is the only reasonable explanation. I don't see any other way it could be dismissed every time an agent or cop got close. I became even more determined to get the Meraz's and anyone connected to their operation.

How was it possible that law enforcement didn't know about the tunnels? Only certain people on our side knew about the tunnels, and they were the corrupt few. Ralph Guzman allowed the Meraz family to smuggle drugs through his tunnels to the United States. I didn't want to get involved with Guzman, so I didn't push it. Life is too short, and there was only so much I was willing to risk.

<><><>

There were four Meraz brothers. One brother was killed earlier, but it's not known how it happened. The other three brothers, Olegario, Oswaldo, and Oscar, were still living in San Luis, Mexico. Oscar was the youngest and most dangerous. He often reacted without thinking. Oswaldo was probably the smartest; he was involved in the community, and his wife was very active in the Catholic church and charity work. Olegario was a produce grower in Mexico and a well-known criminal.

Oswaldo owned a grocery store, a shrimp business, and a restaurant in El Golfo, Mexico. He inherited the shrimp company from Raphael Caro Quintero, a known drug kingpin. Oswaldo was always very polite and well dressed. His son was selected to go to Colorado Springs Air Force Academy for a career as an officer. The brothers knew Arizona State Senator Ed Pastor very well. Senator Pastor was a Hispanic American and supported the agricultural trade in Mexico. He also knew the Meraz's and was familiar with Olegario's produce business. The senator was the one who endorsed Oswaldo's son for the academy. Oswaldo Jr. later dropped out and was arrested at the POE for smuggling marijuana and other unknown reasons. He was released the same day.

According to Mexican officials, the Meraz brothers were very wealthy. They had a weakness: dope and girls. Oscar worked with Olegario and Oswaldo's businesses and was always partying – snorting cocaine and having sex with young Mexican girls brought in for entertainment.

A source well connected to the Meraz's said, "When one of their traffickers lost some dope at the POE, the Meraz brothers made him give up his daughter in exchange for the missing drugs. The daughter was 12-years old and was used by the brothers for sex. When they finished with her, they sent her over to the workers for prostitution." The source asked Larry to help the little girl escape from the brothers. He did his best to try to make that happen but didn't have much luck.

The cartels and drug traffickers would often send girls over to the Meraz home for them to enjoy. This was another reason I was committed to seeing the brothers in prison.

These were the same brothers implicated but never charged in Mexico nor the United States for the 1975 shooting and attempted murder of the two DEA agents, Don Ware and Roy Stevenson.

<><><>

When an American company had a location in Mexico, it was known as the maquiladora. Mexican law required a president of the company to be a Mexican citizen.

Grove Manufacturing was an American company with Grande Manufacturing as its maquiladora. Grande trucks drove to the truck yard at the San Luis border in Arizona, and then Grove trucks would move deliveries within the United States. It was discovered that some employees were receiving kickbacks for allowing Grove/Grande trucks to carry drugs. Enrique Medina-Aquilar was one of those employees. He was the brother-in-law to Oswaldo Meraz and served as the go-between for Grande/Grove

24

Manufacturing and the Meraz organization. As the financial clerk for Grove Manufacturing, Medina was named the president of Grande Manufacturing, the maquiladora.

Aldo Campo worked with Medina as the General Manager of plant operations. He had no familial ties but was as bad as they came – a significant player in the Meraz organization.

Jose Rodriguez Jonas was Olegario Meraz's right-hand man. His family members were high-level mules for the Meraz organization. He was indicted for transporting drugs into Colorado. Jose's sister Irene was married to Juan Medina, Enrique's brother. She was referred to Jeff by a guy in federal prison and became a valuable informant. Irene provided Jeff with useful information and told him about a tunnel the Meraz's used that ran under Friendship Park to a fabric store in San Luis, Arizona.

According to sources and interviews with local law enforcement, the Meraz organization transported marijuana, cocaine, heroin, and sometimes computer chips into the U.S. using other family members working with United States Immigration, Border Patrol, local law enforcement officers, and politicians. Previous cases had been shut down before ever getting to prosecution because of internal leaks.

I felt like I was never going to be successful because of the corruption in the law enforcement community and at the POE at the border of the United States and Mexico. I was facing a challenging problem when sources provided information on corrupt officials in Mexico, and the United States furnished protection and cooperation with the Meraz brothers. I established that the alleged corrupt officials were, most likely, the overriding factor in the Meraz trafficking success in Mexico and the U.S.

Sources, CIs, and the private investigators continued to provide information that the Meraz organization was a cartel controlling the checkpoints along the Arizona and Mexico border. According to the sources, Meraz-Gutierrez brothers in Mexico,

Oswaldo, Olegario, and Oscar, as well as the brother-in-law, Enrique Medina-Aguilar, were all-powerful drug traffickers.

The Meraz brothers had been targets of various federal, state, and local law enforcement investigations since the mid-70s. They were principal organizers and participants in the importation and distribution of large quantities of drugs into the U.S.[36] Using Grande Manufacturing to launder narcotics proceeds with the help of Enrique Medina-Aguilar. Medina was arrested in 1989 for his involvement in transporting several hundred pounds of cocaine seized by United States Customs at the San Luis Port of Entry[37] and later released by the Mexican Federal Police.

I learned from FBI Agent Mark Spencer and other sources about several different run-ins the Meraz's had with law enforcement in Mexico. For example, the Mexican Federal Army once kidnapped Olegario for facilitating a large shipment of heroin. The kidnappers asked for $3 million in USD for Olegario's release.[38]

Spencer showed me a San Luis, Mexican newspaper with Olegario's photo and the story of his kidnapping and ransom fee.

Spencer asked Ralph Guzman, Olegario's partner in the produce business if he was the U.S. contact for Olegario Meraz's narcotic activities. Guzman denied any involvement but was aware of the operations of moving drugs through an underground tunnel into the United States at the San Luis POE. Guzman knew that Olegario was released from his kidnappers, who were the federal police. Oscar paid the ransom to the Mexican Federal agents. Olegario owed the money to the agents for protection to move his dope into the U.S.

Spencer focused on Olegario's kidnapping but didn't provide me with any details about it, even though we were working jointly on the Meraz case. According to Spencer's sources, Oscar now changed his story that the ransom was paid to the Mexican Federal Army for Olegario's release.

In 1991, defendants who worked for the Meraz brothers squealed like rats to law enforcement that Olegario was the owner of more than 500 kilograms of cocaine waiting to move into the states. The defendants also made arrangements for informants to purchase 15-20 kilos of heroin every 15 days to be delivered by Olegario.

Spencer wanted to help with the Meraz investigation and told me I needed FBI money to help buy the dope from the brothers. "You can help me buy 30 kilos of cocaine,"

I told him. With his help, I bought a one-kilo sample of 30 kilos.

<><><>

I started gathering information on how the Meraz's were successful in moving drugs across the border into the United States. I worked by myself, following some of the Meraz's in the Yuma community, the law enforcement community, churches, schools, etc. I followed their cars and trucks, and I followed employees of Grande Manufacturing, keeping a low profile because of law enforcement corruption in the community.

Even though the Meraz's lived across the border in Mexico, they were very active in Yuma and with the church community. They owned homes in Yuma and their relatives and children in Yuma would spy for the families in Mexico. The Meraz daughters targeted law enforcement and used sex to involve them.

At times, I'd work alone across the border in Mexico, checking on Meraz traffickers' residences and vehicles. I wrote down several California license plates, especially at the Olegario Meraz residence. A lot of these license plates were registered to known drug traffickers in the United States.

When employees got off work at Grande Manufacturing in Mexico, I would follow them. Some lived in houses made of plywood. They were definitely not involved in drug trafficking. And yet, the Grande company owner was making millions off the backs of Mexicans making 50¢ or $1 an hour. I planned to make an example of the maquiladora and what the owners were doing.

I searched many produce trucks, most of them 18-wheelers, coming across at the San Luis POE. Grove trucks were among them. When I got information from my informants or sources that there might be drugs on a truck, I'd stop and search it. I was more fueled, now that Jeff and Randy were involved. I wanted those in Mexico to know that I, DEA Agent Larry Hardin, was going to seize their dope and trucks at the border.

I learned from sources and law enforcement investigators that the Meraz's were behind shipments of drugs coming across the border on produce trucks from the Grande warehouse.

I got a call from Frank Grover, the owner of Grove/Grande Manufacturing out of Los Angeles, "Larry, I heard you're stopping some of my trucks coming across at San Luis."

I didn't say much.

As it turned out, Frank Grover, owner of Grove and Grande Manufacturing companies, was not aware of the situation in Mexico. When he heard about the use of his trucks for drug trafficking, he wanted to put a stop to it. Immediately! This was not something he wanted to be associated with his company. We agreed. If I could seize one of these trucks, I might be able to put a stop to this for him.

Chapter 4: Grove Manufacturing

1991, Los Angeles, CA

About the same time, Larry was beginning his investigation of the Meraz organization, and the Pearce Corporation was beginning their investigation on behalf of Grove Manufacturing.

Jeff Pearce and Randy Torgerson worked for Jerry Pearce and would testify in Agent Larry Hardin's DEA case when the time came. But when they got started on the case in early 1993, they didn't know Larry or have a clue as to how big and dangerous the case was going to become.

In 1991, Pearce Corporation was hired by the management of Grove Manufacturing to uncover improprieties from within the company. Jeff started working in Los Angeles and became the main investigator in Yuma and San Luis, Arizona. Randy did most of his work in Los Angeles and often worked with John. Erik, another investigator in the Pearce Corporation, usually worked with Jeff in Yuma, and occasionally, Randy or John would join Jeff.

Grove Manufacturing was founded in 1947 by Frank's father and uncle, Richard Grover and Richard's brother, Paul. Coincidentally, that was the same year the CIA was founded. Randy thought, *We're sure it's only a coincidence.*

Grove manufactures furniture, primarily out of Hawthorne, California. Initially, there were plants located in California, Arkansas, and Mexico. The case started with Richard Grover, and after he died in December 1991, we continued working with his sons, Frank and Bill. Frank became president of the company while he and his brother were primary shareholders. Michael Weber was on the board of directors and also a primary shareholder.

In 1991-92, Frank Grover became suspicious of his brother, Bill when he began liquidating his shares of stock, and he wasn't selling them to Michael or Frank. Bill was in high management at Grove Manufacturing. Frank suspected he might be involved with drugs, and he didn't want any of that in his company. He knew Bill ordered a lot of products from China that were delivered directly to his home, and Frank couldn't understand what that was about, but he was suspicious.

Frank had the company's inside counsel reach out to their outside counsel – Gibson, Dunn, & Crutcher, a large law firm in Century City with additional offices in downtown Los Angeles, Europe, and across the country.[39] He inquired about needing private investigators to coordinate information and find out what his brother was up to.

One of the partners had worked with Jerry Pearce in the past and asked him if he could help Frank Grover.

Jerry contacted Frank Grover and took on the case. He asked Jeff to watch Bill Grover's activities. Later, he brought Randy and John in to continue gathering information about Bill's activities.

<><><>

Randy

Bill Grover lived in a nice house in the hills of Palos Verdes, California. John and I watched the house and Bill's coming and going at the corporate office in San Pedro. We wanted to see who he was meeting. John and I became very focused on what Bill Grover would need to be delivered directly to his home. We tried to get as much detail as we could. It had to be something illegal that he didn't want anyone else at the company to know, or so we thought. One day John and I saw several boxes being delivered to his home. When we looked through binoculars, or "long eyes" as we used to call them; we could see into the window of one of the rooms where there were several stacks of boxes.

We decided to find out what was in those boxes. More than likely, different from what was on the manifest. We were doing this surveillance right after the earthquake, and we decided to go into Bill's house, posing as a security company sniffing for gas leaks.

Bill's wife answered the door. "We're working in the area looking for gas leaks. Could we come in and check the house?"

We had some makeshift equipment. Nothing that did anything, but it all looked official, so we could sniff around. John kept Bill's wife busy while I went into the room to look in the boxes. I opened a few boxes and could see they had a lot of tennis balls. There were a lot of boxes, and I couldn't open every one of them. I didn't know if there was anything inside those tennis balls and couldn't spend more time finding out. I didn't want to get caught. So, that was all we could report.

We got out of there, and nobody was ever the wiser. At least we found out what was in there. It's not clear why Bill Grover needed so many tennis balls. What was he going to do with them? The explanation must have satisfied them because they didn't go any further with it. I was very disappointed!

Jeff also had information that Bill was involved with drugs. The PIs thought maybe there were some drugs or paraphernalia in those boxes. Later, we discovered that Bill just had a side hustle, but no real explanation. So, who knows…?

<><><>

Meetings with the Grovers

At one of the first times the private investigators met with Frank Grover, Jerry mentioned, "We discovered that several years ago Grove trucks were being used to transport drugs."

Frank was naturally very concerned. Previously, he had hired a private investigator named James Lawrence to see if he could learn anything about the supposed drugs. "I thought Lawrence investigated that at the time and couldn't find any proof to connect our company to drugs. Now it's coming up again? Are you telling me heroin and cocaine are being transported on our trucks? We could lose most of our business if anyone found drugs connected to us. We must do something right away! This needs to end!"

Jerry told him, "We'll investigate it further. We'll need to get as much information as we can and find out if it's still happening."

He turned to Jeff and said, "I want you and John to go down to Yuma to watch the Grove trucks coming across at San Luis Port of Entry."

Frank Grover met with the rest of the Pearce Corporation and briefed them on the situation and the investigation that had been done previously.

In the beginning, Grove Manufacturing's three California locations were Los Angeles, Hawthorne, and Gardena. Gardena was headquarters for administration, manufacturing, and the distribution warehouse. Everything was moved into one large facility in Hawthorne halfway through the case

In 1987, FBI contacted Richard Grover about the Meraz organization using the company's trucks to transport drugs. They told him they believed Grove trucks were transporting heroin and cocaine, and if he worked with FBI, they wouldn't confiscate his trucks – approximately 200 semi-trucks across the country.

Richard Grover told the FBI, "We don't want our trucks taken, and we don't knowingly involve drugs in our work. So, yes, absolutely, we'll cooperate with you!"

Private investigator James Lawrence had a lot of the players' names and some notes on the Blue Finn Seafood Company in California. He saw that Grove Manufacturing was transporting shrimp loads from Oswaldo Meraz and Raphael Quintero and delivering them to Blue Finn. He didn't find out anything about drugs. Lawrence's case was closed because he couldn't verify a drug connection. That didn't occur until the Pearce Corporation were involved.

The Pearce Corporation began to confirm the information they learned from Frank Grover about the company and previous issues with their trucks.

<><><>

Dianne

In his research, Randy found dealings were going back to the '70s and '80s, to the time of the Iran Contra affair. At the time,

Michael Weber was one of the senior vice presidents of Grove Manufacturing, and Jeff and Randy believed, but couldn't prove, that Weber had a part in letting the movement of weapons take place. Weber was a friend of Oliver North. It was assumed that North asked Weber if some of the trucks could be used to take weapons into Mexico. Weber went to a lot of parties with Oliver North back then, so it stands to reason he was connected in some way.

Frank, more so than his dad, Richard, really wanted to get to the bottom of things. When Richard passed away, Grove Manufacturing renewed their commitment to the work the Pearce Corporation to look further into exactly what the trucks were transporting.

They found that during the time Clinton was governor of Arkansas, 1979-1981 and 1983-1992, people at the Grove Manufacturing plant were observed loading guns on Grove Manufacturing trailers. The trucks were escorted down across the border through San Luis POE. The escorts turned out to be the cartel. The private investigators discovered it was indeed the Meraz cartel guarding the transport of guns across the border and deep into Mexico. The connection was finally established.

<><><>

San Luis, Mexico & Mena, AR

In the 1980s, the Meraz's were probably the third-largest drug cartel in Mexico.[40] On March 16, 1986, President Ronald Reagan spoke on national television with a plea for restoring congressional aide to the Nicaraguan Contras. The United States supplied weapons to the Contras and escorted them across the border through Mexico to Nicaragua. Barry Seal was one of the pilots who transported weapons in exchange for drugs.[41]

Seal worked with the CIA in the 1960s when he was a pilot in the U.S. Army's Special Forces. He was busted by U.S. Customs while working as a commercial pilot for Trans World Airlines for attempting to smuggle explosives into Mexico for a group of

Cubans against Castro. He lost his job with the airlines, but was protected by his connections with the CIA.[42]

Seal began flying his private planes. He was known as a top drug smuggler and dealer for Pablo Escobar's Medellin Cartel. He coordinated and smuggled cocaine and marijuana with his private plane, beginning from his operations in Louisiana. In 1982 with the CIA's help, he moved his airstrip and operations to Mena, Arkansas. The DEA caught him in the early '80s and flipped him to work for them. They allowed him to continue flying drugs and money, to see where everything was going and where it was coming from.[43] This led to Seal being known as "the most important witness in the history of U.S. Drug Enforcement Administration."[44]

This was one of the ways they caught on to Manuel Noriega's drug running. Oliver North's big claim to fame in his career was the Iran Contra Affair that involved Manuel Noriega in Panama.[45] DEA was in a unique position to see where many pieces of the puzzle were coming together. They were able to connect a lot, but, didn't actually put it all together.[46] In the 1980s, Seal "became one of the most important and daring undercover operatives, infiltrating the top Colombian drug operations...Seal was scheduled to be the key witness against...Jorge Ochoa, the top Colombian drug boss...in jail in Spain, [who was] about to be extradited to the United States."[47] He was then relieved from his connections with the DEA.[48]

Seal flew his private planes from Mena to cartel airstrips in Colombia and Venezuela with supplies and guns for CIA operations. On the return trip to Mena, he would refuel in Panama and Honduras and while flying over the farms on Seal's property would drop parachutes attached to bags of cocaine for cartel distributors in the U.S.[49]

Two of the Cartel members he worked with were Jorge Ochoa and Frederico Vaughn, who were close associates of the Sandinistas. Frederico Vaughn's cousin, Barney Vaughn worked for the Popular Bank and Trust Company. This was the bank used

34

by the CIA and Oliver North when they were working with the Contras.[50]

Barry Seal lived on property managed by the Rose Law Firm, where Hilary Clinton was working. It was Bill Clinton who called to get him released. Clinton's brother was involved with Tyson Chicken, also in Arkansas. His brother was a known dope user.[51]

Later, Seal was caught and sentenced to five years in a Florida prison.

In 1986, after serving only three years, he transitioned to a halfway house in Baton Rouge, Louisiana. "He'd been told that the Medellin Cartel, run by Colombian drug lords and Pablo Escobar, had put a $500,000 bounty on his head after his status as an informant had been leaked to the press by the Reagan-Bush administration."[52]

Seal "was a victim of Oliver North's press leaks."[53] He was well-connected with the CIA, and they used him. He's the one who paid the price, not the agents or others involved. They went on in their careers. [54]

Seal was murdered in 1986 by five men with machine-guns, ordered by Jorge Ochoa and Pablo Escobar when he was waiting to testify for the government. Seal was in the witness protection program and sitting in his car outside the house.[55]

<> <> <>

On Kiki Camarena's case, the trial records included so many files and tapes it took Randy three months, eight hours a day, five days a week to go through them in the archives at downtown Los Angeles Court House.

"There were five to seven stacks of files that went from floor to ceiling. That's how big this case file was, many pages! It was crazy! There were phone records, notes, and surveillance reviews tying people to those in the Meraz case in the 1990s."[56]

Everybody knows when an agent gets hurt or killed, and all the red flags go up on the border. It's an unwritten rule that a killing is either by accident or by permission. It's like in the old Godfather days with the Mafia. You don't whack a cop unless you get permission, and everybody knows because the FBI and DEA will be coming for you.[57]

Bob Wiedrich of the *Chicago Tribune* stated, "Any time day or night, DEA agents are risking their lives somewhere in the world, carrying out their duties with professional competence and dedication often far beyond the call of duty. They do not appreciate Jackson's derogatory comments...Neither should the American people who have the greatest stake of all in the deadly serious job of fighting the international drug traffic."[58]

<><><>

In 1985, Mexico City suffered a violent earthquake with a magnitude of 8.0. Serious damage affected the greater Mexico City area with deaths of at least 5,000 people. The torture tapes of Kiki Camarena were held in the State Department's office in Mexico City where they were officially destroyed in the quake.

Randy thought, Officially? Yeah, right!

Years before the kidnapping, Kiki Camarena had been a friend of Jerry Pearce, owner of Pearce Corporation.

Pearce Corporation discovered that when Bill Clinton was Arkansas Governor and Hillary Clinton worked at the Rose Law Firm, some of the rebels supported in Nicaragua secretly trained on property managed by the Rose Law Firm in Mena, Arkansas. This was near the Grove Manufacturing large distribution plant.[59] The investigators, trying to connect the dots, concluded that much of this activity was happening based on what their informants provided.

When the weapons were being moved from the United States overseas, the U.S. government had to come up with a route to get the guns into Mexico without being noticed. What the private investigators didn't know, but surmised to be accurate, was the connection was with the CIA.

Facts were limited about the cartel guarding weapons going to Nicaragua. However, who else would oversee that? Later, at a meeting with the United States Attorney's office in Phoenix, an unknown gentleman, believed to be CIA, ended up taking the case files back to Langley, Virginia. So, the team was pretty sure the CIA had a hand in it. On Christmas Eve 1992, President Bush issued pardons to all those indicted in the scandal. The Iran-Contra Affair had ended.

The Pearce Corporation started the case almost one year before the Iran-Contra program ended. The government investigation of it went on for years. Their information was timely. They just didn't know it yet.

<>><><>

Los Angeles, CA
Jeff

Jerry got upset with something Jeff did in Yuma. He told Jeff, "You go work with Randy for this week. I'm not sending you back to Yuma right now."

So, Randy brought me with him to Torrance to look for theft of furniture and odd deliveries or stops by Grove trucks, but it was more about watching Ray Grover. Randy and I got along great and had fun when we were worked together. Randy was generally happy, and I had just gone through a difficult time in Yuma.

In Los Angeles, we all stayed in Marina del Rey. Jerry had a 32-34 ft. yacht. That was our base of operation in L.A., for the most part. Randy probably stayed there the most of anyone.

Jerry was on the yacht when the Northridge earthquake happened. Randy and I were on a plane heading down there that morning. It was strange! When we got to Marina del Rey, we went with Jerry to breakfast. There were some big after-shocks while we were sitting in a restaurant. We watched the ground open up by the beach!

When we got back on the boat, Randy and I told Jerry we were going to Torrance, He asked, "What are you guys going to do down there?"

"We're going to watch the *Blue Finn Seafood Company*," and jumped in the car.

One of the offices was under the 10 Freeway. Randy and I were sitting down the street. In Yuma, I was used to moving and shaking all the time. Sitting in a car was not my ideal type of work. I would do surveillance, but I wasn't very patient.

I decided I wanted to do something, so I said to Randy, "Let's go in!"

"What? What?"

"I said let's go in. Let's pose as workman's comp investigators. We're going to do a claims investigation."

Randy wasn't sure what I had in mind, but said, "Ok."

We pulled the car up closer to the building and walked in. There was a desk at the front as we came in the door, just outside the warehouse. It was manned by Lan Bao Yang, one of the brothers who spoke English. He was the only one there who spoke English. I recognized Lan Ming immediately because I had seen a photograph. I looked at Randy, but Randy didn't know who this guy was.

I said, "I'm here from Workman's Comp because someone had an injury."

Lan said, "I don't know what you're talking about."

"We're here to do a claim investigation."

"Let me go check with . . . "

There were some boxes next to the desk. A red book that looked like a personal phone book was on top of the boxes. There was another one, brand new, on the desk. Lan was probably transferring information to his new phone book.

I was yelling because the women in the office didn't understand me. As I was talking, my arms were going up and down and, suddenly, at one point, when my arms came up, I had the book in my hand.

Randy didn't say anything at that moment, but his eyes popped out. He was watching me and quietly whispered, "What are you doing?"

"Just wait a second."

Lan came back and said, "We don't have any record of anybody getting hurt."

So, I started pointing my hand with the book in it at Lan as I talked, "Look, you're not wasting my time coming out here."

Pointing the book at him. Lan didn't realize it was his book! "I'll figure out what's going on and I'll call you. Do you have a number?"

Lan gave us a number, and I said, "I'll call and make an appointment."

"Yes, please do!"

We both walked out, and I still had the book in my hand. Randy said, "Jeff, you didn't walk in there with that."

Randy started to speed up as he was walking to get in front of me. He was almost trotting, not really running, but walking really fast.

I told him, "Walk! Look natural!"

When we got in the car, Randy asked, "What did you just do?"

"I took a book! It's an asset relocation."

I started flipping through the pages and went directly to the "M's." "I'm looking for the Meraz's." I found a listing for "Meraz Brothers" and started going through the pages.

I told Randy as I started seeing numbers to the state department. "Who do they know at the State Department?" I also found the name Hugo Salazar, the CIA operative working for *Blue Finn Seafood Company*.

Another interesting name that was in the news quite a lot was John Huang. Huang went to the White House often to meet with

Bill Clinton.[60] He was at the center of an investigation for raising funds for the Democratic National Committee (DNC) during the 1992 Presidential election. Several significant campaign contributions came through China, Taiwan, Korea, Vietnam, and Indonesia and had to be returned. Legally, the money cannot come "from foreign citizens or businesses unless the donors reside in the United States or the money comes from an American subsidiary."[61]

We went back to the boat where Jerry was waiting for us. Jerry never leaves anywhere where food is readily available. He doesn't travel too far away from the food.

Jerry looked at us and said, "What are you assholes doing back so early?"

"Well, you asked me why I came down here. Here!" and I handed him the red book.

"What is that?"

"*Blue Finn Seafood Company*, Lan Bao Yang's phone book!"

"How in the fuck did you get that?"

Jerry was flipping through the book and said, "No! Wow! . . ." He was getting excited. His eyes are getting wider. It was shortly after that; I received a letter from Jerry of a job well-done. It was the only time I got a letter like that from my uncle.

We also gave Larry a copy of the book because it included names of government officials, senators, and others that might help his case.

Chapter 5: Larry Develops a CI; San Luis, AZ & San Luis, Mexico

1991, Larry

In late summer of 1991, I decided I needed to find a Confidential Informant (CI) to help uncover what was going on with the Meraz organization.

I needed a way into their organization, starting at the top. You just can't walk in and ask for drugs from the brothers. You can do that at the street level, but it's no way to penetrate the top. Cartel leaders would never talk drugs with undercover cops or informants. They're well protected and insulated by the "family" and corruption in law enforcement.

I knew it was all about the money! Money played a role in both sides of the border, and someone in law enforcement or maybe our government was keeping the Meraz's out of jail in Mexico and the United States.

I told my wife I wasn't afraid of the criminals in Yuma or Mexico, but if I were killed, it would be a corrupt cop, a United States Customs or Immigration Inspector who pulled the trigger. I had lost two co-workers, killed by a Yuma County Deputy Sheriff, a corrupt cop who was a retired Marine Staff Sergeant working on OCDETF cases.

I called my main office in Phoenix and told them, "I need to develop a CI who doesn't live in Yuma or down in San Luis. Most local cops and sources know everyone in the Yuma County area, and I needed to bring in someone with their own legitimate produce business or any other business, hopefully outside of Arizona."

"What kind of informant do you need?"

"Someone classy and well-dressed who doesn't look like a doper. He needs to have his own business. Preferably in the U.S."

While waiting for an informant from Phoenix, I started meeting with Jeff, John, and Randy regularly when they were in

Yuma. Later on, they included Erik. Jeff spent much of his time in Yuma, surveilling the connections there and in Mexico. They provided a lot of information to me about the Meraz operation with the Grove/Grande trucks and corrupt law enforcement in Yuma County. It was unbelievable how these guys got their information. They gave me the name of Enrique Medina, and that made the connection for me and thanks to their help, the case took off. Their boss, Jerry, and I communicated a lot over the phone.

Several weeks later, I got a call from an agent at DEA headquarters. "We found someone who owns a shrimp business down in Hermosillo, Mexico. He's a reliable source who's helped us with some good drug cases in the U.S. and south of the border. However, he has a cocaine problem and screws anything that moves. DEA arrested him for cocaine trafficking in the United States and served five years in federal prison. He was recently released from prison and had a felony record for trafficking drugs. He's from Colombia, originally from Peru."

It takes a crook to do a crook. Wow! Now, I can have a reliable source owning a shrimp business in Mexico operating in the Meraz's own backyard.

I told him, "Okay, that's perfect! I'd like to meet with him."

The source contacted me a few days later, and I invited him to Yuma so we could meet in person. I wanted to see what he looked like and the way he dressed. It was also crucial for me to let him tell me about who he was and what he did. This was my way of learning how truthful he was and if I could trust him.

When we met for the first time, he drove up to the restaurant in a very nice car. He was wearing slacks and a polo shirt; very classy, well educated, and spoke excellent English with a heavy accent. I could tell he came from a good background and was educated.

I said, "You don't look like a Mexican."

"I'm not. I'm Colombian."

"You're Colombian?"

"Yep, I'm from Bogota, Colombia. I have my own shrimp business."

Everything was going great, and I was trying not to get too excited. He was very polite and easygoing, and everything he told me was validated by what I already knew about him.

"What's your background? Why do you want to work for us?"

"I did a lot of cocaine and made a lot of money several years ago. One time I made a phone call to an agent working undercover. They arrested me, and I went to federal prison for five years for conspiracy and trafficking cocaine."

I was thinking: *Yeah, there's more involved here, but I kept my suspicions to myself.* "But you're out of prison now and working for us. Look, this is what I want you to do. I want you to work for me, and I want to see what you can do."

"I live in Phoenix, but I do go back and forth to Bogota to check on my shrimp business. There's this other guy you might know who lives down Mexico. His name is Mario Camaron."

"Never heard of him."

"He also has a shrimp business in Mexico."

"Okay, if you want to work for me, I'll pay you, but you come under my direction. If you get hurt, you'll get disability for the rest of your life. In other words, you're a part of the DEA family, and we're very serious about that. I'm going to call you, Pedro, is that okay with you?"

"Sure."

"This is what we've got going on, Pedro."

I explained to him that I required his loyalty and outlined some things about the trucks I was watching at the border. "I have the name Enrique Medina-Aguilar. I want you to give him a call and see if he'll meet with you. He works at Grande, a maquiladora process factory that makes furniture in Mexico. I'd like you to meet with him if you can. Give him a call and see what happens, okay? You and Enrique have something in common. Women! Tell him you met him at El Tigre Bar in Tijuana. You own a business in Mexico and want to move shrimp into the United States. Talk about women." I added emphatically, "Pedro, you can't use drugs working with DEA. Got it?"

I gave him Enrique's contact information. El Tigre Bar is a popular place where dopers meet in Tijuana, Mexico. I knew from what I learned from the private investigators and my own surveillance that Medina socialized with the Meraz's and went back and forth between their homes in Mexico. I didn't mention the Meraz's to Pedro. I wasn't sure how Enrique related to them until I heard it from Jeff.

I knew what it took for Pedro to get information and stay alive. Every cop tells their CIs not to commit crimes or do anything that might jeopardize the case. Under normal circumstances, CIs can get away with some things. But this was no ordinary case!

Pedro made the call to Grande and spoke to Enrique in Spanish. "Hey, I met you down at the bar in Tijuana, at El Tigre Bar. We met there and got to talking about women. I mentioned my shrimp business, and you said you know someone else who has a shrimp business."

Enrique bit! He said to Pedro, "Come on down, I'd like to meet with you." He gave Pedro the address for Grande Manufacturing in San Luis Rio Colorado, Mexico.

A few days later, Pedro called me, "I told him we met, and I wanted to meet his friend with the shrimp business. He told me to come to San Luis at the place where he worked."

I was thinking: This was too good to be true! I knew from Jeff that Enrique is the brother-in-law of one of the Meraz's.

Within a few days, Pedro called and said he had a meeting with Enrique at Grande Manufacturing in Mexico.

Under my instruction, Pedro went to San Luis, Mexico, alone and met with Enrique. They drank and did some dope, although I didn't know about that part of it at the time.

Enrique told Pedro, "I want to introduce you to my friend Oswaldo, who owns a shrimp business in San Luis."

"Yes, I'd like to meet him. When can we meet?"

"I'll get back to you."

After Pedro and Enrique snorted a few lines of cocaine, Enrique told Pedro that Oswaldo transported a lot of shrimp. Enrique laughed as he continued, "Even cocaine and heroin to Los Angeles, California."

<><><>

A few days later, after Pedro had gone into Mexico, he called me. "I met with Enrique. He drinks a lot, and the more he snorts, the more he talks. He told me his brother-in-law is Oswaldo Meraz. I think he said, Meraz. Anyway, he wants to meet about making some extra money."

Pedro learned Oswaldo owns a shrimp business in El Golfo and a grocery store. And Oswaldo's older brother is a guy by the name of Olegario.

I was listening very carefully, and I couldn't believe it was everything I'd hoped for: He met with Enrique who told him about Oswaldo with a shrimp business. I played my poker face and didn't show any emotion. I knew he was talking about the Meraz brothers.

I told him, "Okay, let's give it a few days. Then call him back and tell him you'd like to meet Oswaldo. You want to talk to him about your shrimp business."

Pedro asked, "Who's this guy, Oswaldo?"

"You'll learn what kind of a person he is soon. Stay focused and be safe."

I had finally found a weak link through Enrique to get to the Meraz family. My first thought was, Thank you, Jeff, Randy, and the other Pearce Investigators because you gave me Enrique's name. It's paying off big time!

I knew what was going on because Pedro had to advise me whenever he went to Mexico. That was for his safety, and he was very good about keeping me informed.

Pedro told me they would meet at a store in San Luis that Oswaldo owned. I knew nothing about this store. They would discuss their shrimp business and nothing else. The Meraz's won't talk dope with just anyone. You have to be a family member or a very trusted individual before they would even mention their drug activities.

Pedro told me he believed Enrique was living the "Great Life" in Yuma and Mexico as the general manager of a maquiladora and able to do pretty much what he wanted.

When I met with Pedro later, he told me, "You know, Larry, that port of entry down there, something isn't right. They're asking me questions."

"What kind of questions?"

"They're asking what's going on, why I'm going into Mexico, what I was doing in San Luis. I had my Colombian passport and my visa and told them I live in Phoenix, Arizona."

"You didn't slip up, did you?"

"No, I just told them I own a shrimp business in Mexico, and I come back and forth."

"Okay, okay. Just be very cautious with the people at the San Luis Port of Entry. Especially with law enforcement there. I'm not talking about the Mexicans; I'm talking about the United States side when you come into the country."

"Okay. Oswaldo asked me if I could get him some dope out of Colombia. I think this guy might be a dealer."

"You think so?"

"Yeah, I do."

"What's going to happen next?"

"He wants to meet again."

"Ok, go for it."

I wanted Pedro to give Oswaldo something he could use for his business that would also help us. Like some new communication radios for his shrimp boats with listening devices in them. I could keep tabs on the Meraz organization and what they were doing on their boats in El Golfo.

I told Pedro, "Ask Oswaldo if he needs new radios for his shrimp boats."

The next time Pedro met with Oswaldo, he asked.

Oswaldo said he could use them because the ones he had weren't working very well.

Pedro told Oswaldo he'd have the radios in a couple of weeks.

I reached out to a United States Customs Agent and part of the OCDETF team that I trusted. "I need new boat radios for my case. Can you provide them from surplus?" I told them about the shrimp boats coming out of El Golfo, Mexico and that I wanted to track them because they're bringing narcotics into the U.S.

"I can get you four of the radios you need. Somebody will call you to set it up."

When I got the call, they told me, "We can implant listening devices in the radios. When someone pushes down to talk, we can hear their conversations and where they're calling from. We'll get these shipped out to you this week."

This was great technology at the time and could help me figure out what these guys were doing.

I kept my supervisor updated and handed the radios over to Pedro.

Pedro told Oswaldo he had the radios, and they went down to meet him in El Golfo.

Oswaldo really liked getting the radios for his shrimp boats and found them very useful for his men. "Are you sure I can't pay for these?" he asked.

"No, these are a gift from me." I had told Pedro not to accept any payment.

A customs agent told me they had someone from U.S. Customs Maritime Intelligence tracking Oswaldo's boats and their communications. The following week, I was told they followed a message that one of Oswaldo's shrimp boats met with an unknown Colombian boat in the waters off El Golfo. After I heard about this conversation, I never received any further information about Oswaldo's boats. For unknown reasons, they stopped providing information to the customs agent who was sharing with me.

I knew Pedro needed protection when he met the Meraz's and their associates in Mexico. He was one of the best informants I'd ever had. I had to find another CI to drive and protect Pedro when he met with Oswaldo or his brothers. As a business owner operating in Mexico, it didn't look right that he didn't have a bodyguard. It would also be helpful to have another witness to testify against the Meraz's. Informants typically testify in cases they've been involved with, but they're not mentioned by name in court to protect their identity and keep them safe.

I told Pedro to find someone to drive him back and forth from Mexico. Someone to protect him down there. Someone he could rely on. If something happened, I couldn't help him. And I didn't want to know if the guy carried a gun.

Pedro told me, "Okay, I think I know someone."

Three or four weeks later, Pedro called, "I have someone, he's Colombian. That's where I met him. I really trust this guy. I think he'll take excellent care of me."

This was perfect. For some reason, Mexicans don't like Colombians, but they like their drugs, especially their cocaine.

"Ok, bring him out to Yuma and let me meet him."

I met him, he was really short, probably about five feet tall, husky build, really quiet, and didn't talk much. He said very little when I asked him questions. If he wasn't a criminal, he fooled me.

He appeared to be very humble, yet able to kill quickly if necessary. Could I trust him? If this guy couldn't kill the criminal, he would go after the criminal's family.

Pedro trusted this guy with his life and wanted him to be his bodyguard and driver. They trusted each other. They were

48

Colombians dealing drugs with Mexicans. There was no love lost between Colombian and Mexican drug smugglers.

His name was Enano, "Enano, you're going work with us. You're going to stick with me, and I want you to stay close to Pedro. Don't snort drugs or carry a gun. Do you understand me?"

"Yes," Enano responded.

So, he was going to be Pedro's driver and bodyguard. Would he be armed every time he went into Mexico? If he weren't, he'd be stupid.

I looked at both Pedro and Enano and told them, "Let's go after these guys!"

Pedro and Enano didn't know the Meraz's were behind the attempted murder of the two DEA agents in 1975. The Meraz name was never mentioned to Pedro and Enano because I couldn't give my sources that information.

The next time Pedro and Enano met with Oswaldo, he told them he wanted to introduce them to his younger brother, Oscar. The meeting was set up for the next day in El Golfo, a little fishing village off the coast, a three-hour drive south from the San Luis POE.

I met with Pedro at a coffee shop in Yuma.

"Oswaldo is pleased with the radios. He wants me to see if I can get more. Larry, this guy Oswaldo, is going to introduce me to his younger brother, Oscar."

Of course, I knew who Oscar was. Everybody in Yuma knew who he was: a very bad dude.

"Who's Oscar, Pedro?"

"I don't know; he told me he's his younger brother."

"I think Oswaldo and his brothers are dangerous people."

"Oswaldo's shrimp processing plant and employees are unsanitary, but it's not a legitimate shrimp business. He's just using it as a cover for their drug operations."

Oswaldo was now willing to discuss drugs with Pedro. He wanted him to meet his brother, Oscar, to start smuggling cocaine in his shrimp into the United States. He told Pedro not to worry about the border into San Luis, Arizona.

I knew Oswaldo Meraz had a shrimp business that exported beautiful tiger shrimp. It was a legitimate business in El Golfo, Mexico. Now I was getting excited about Oswaldo because the name was coming to me from both directions, CIs and the private investigators.

In a couple of weeks, Pedro met Oswaldo again with Enano at his side. This time they were very relaxed and decided to meet again in El Golfo so Oswaldo could show him his shrimp business. It's about an hour-and-a-half or two-hour drive south of the border.

The next time when they met in El Golfo, Jose Jonas Rodrigues joined them. Jose was Olegario's right-hand man. His wife was a schoolteacher and ran the DARE program in Yuma County. Jose also had relatives working at the POE. He was extremely connected; every time Pedro and Enano met with Oswaldo, Jose was there.

Larry met with Pedro and Enano the next day.

"Pedro, who did Oswaldo have you meet with?" I asked.

Pedro told me, "I met with Oscar and another guy by the name of Olegario." Pedro surmised that Oswaldo, Oscar, and Olegario Meraz were extremely powerful and dangerous in Mexico.

"At the meeting, they asked Enano and me several times about producing coca and smuggling cocaine paste from Colombia into San Luis, Mexico. Oscar said he could sell me hydrochloric acid and ether for cocaine production. And Oswaldo said he has the right connection at the San Luis Port of Entry to smuggle anything, even aliens! Oscar told us he's known as the 'King of Heroin' and Olegario Meraz is called the 'King of Cocaine' in Mexico."

Bingo! I could see this all coming together, and my sources and information were becoming verified. In order to put the Meraz's in jail, I had to have the facts. Pedro was going to meet with Oswaldo again to discuss their shrimp business, and I was getting closer to catching the Meraz's.

<><><>

Now I needed to concentrate on factual evidence and not just hearsay or intelligence evidence.

Michael Hope was taken off the case. He was reassigned over to another federal agency. Another attorney, AUSA Richard Dreamer, was assigned to the case. He was a character; the guy never worked any drugs cases before, only white-collar sex crimes against children. Now he was assigned to an incredible case. It took someone who knew how to do cases like these to work this one. So I had to start all over again with him.

AUSA Dreamer, and later AUSA Jimmie Lost, refused to prosecute on conspiracy alone. I had to catch the brothers doing something criminally wrong, not in Mexico, but in the United States.

I was getting excited. Pedro continued to confirm the involvement of Oswaldo, Oscar, and their associates.

I was learning more about the Meraz's. Oscar was a punk who gave no mercy when it came to anything – corruption, hurting people, whatever. If he wanted someone, he would go after them and their family. On one occasion, he told DEA at the American Consulate Office in Hermosillo, Mexico that his brother Olegario was the drug trafficker, not him.

The Meraz's were known for supplying drugs and women, not so much for killing. They had people to do their killing for them. It was always that way.

Later, Pedro and Enano met with Oscar and Olegario at a large white house in San Luis, Mexico. When they reported back to me, they said, "It looks like the White House, except smaller. There were a lot of guys walking around, armed, and watching us as we met with the brothers."

They said that Oswaldo lived across the street in another large white house. It also looked like the U.S. White House.

For two days, Pedro and Enano were locked up in Olegario's house, snorting cocaine with the brothers. Women would come and go from the house. Pedro and I weren't in contact because he was being watched very carefully. Olegario asked if Pedro and Enano were DEA. Then Olegario started laughing and said, "I'm kidding. DEA can't do drugs or have sex with young girls. They can't have sex at all when they're working."

Later Oscar told Pedro and Enano his brothers tried to kill two DEA agents.

Oscar asked the sources, "Are you DEA agents? There will be no doubt, next time!" Oscar was amused and laughed when he said this.

Then he asked Pedro and Enano, "Do you know Johnny Perez? He owns a car dealership in Yuma. Olegario purchased vehicles from Johnny for $135,000 in exchange for drugs back in November 1992."

Laughing, he said, "You should buy a car from Perez."

Johnny Perez was highly connected with the Meraz's. He was the Mayor of San Luis, Arizona. He was a corrupt used-car-dealer and a rapist in Yuma.

Olegario boasted about his friends and family working at the Port of Entry and his connections with the CIA. He said his niece had access to the law enforcement databases on computers at the POE that showed who was looking at her family and Olegario's traffickers. She also knew when DEA agents were targeting the Meraz trucks and cars and could find out about the sources working for DEA. Pedro and Enano were terrified the brothers would find out they were working with me.

Olegario also mentioned he had a nephew working at the Port of Entry, but never said his name. The more Olegario snorted coke, the more he ran his mouth. He never stopped bragging about how he could never be arrested because of his relationship with the CIA.

Oscar shared a lot of stories with Pedro and Enano. He told them that when Americans go to Mexico, his Mexican police buddies separate a husband or boyfriend from a woman if she's "hot." They take the woman to the back room and have sex with her. After they finish with her, she's strongly encouraged not to mention what happened to anyone, or she and husband or boyfriend will disappear or be charged with a violation.

"In San Luis, this was just a way of life for the women," said Oscar. "It's known that Mexican women always carry a bottle of Vaseline with them for lubrication because they never know if they're going to have sex with a police officer or two. They need the Vaseline because they want to be able to walk normally."

Oscar added, "American women never carry Vaseline. That's why they bleed a lot." Then he laughed and said, "In the United States they call it 'Rape.'"

At Olegario's house, there was a band room with a stage for big gatherings. That was where they held beauty pageants for the Mexican Corona beer girls. Pedro and Enano snorted cocaine with Oscar and Olegario and had sex whenever they wanted with the girls who came through.

Olegario knew if Pedro and Enano were DEA agents, they would have already arrested them, right there on the spot. The CIs always told the brothers they weren't DEA. Even when Oscar pointed his .45-caliber at their heads and smiled, Pedro denied his DEA involvement and insisted he only wanted to make some easy money in the states. Oscar responded, "That's your job, a DEA agent!" Enano watched Pedro and Oscar closely.

"We're in!" Pedro told me. "It's only a matter of time until we can start buying drugs."

Now Pedro and Enano were involved, and they started getting free samples of coke to snort with the Meraz brothers. They were making the connections I needed, and I was building the case.

I was thinking: This is it! It's what I've hoped for. Everything's taking shape now!

Pedro and Enano had no idea how important Olegario was. I was excited that they were with the brothers inside Olegario's home, but I insisted they needed to stop snorting coke.

This was exciting! One more Meraz brother. Now, I had all three in my sights, thanks to Pedro and Enano.

My informants had a gut feeling the Meraz's had protection from law enforcement at the POE. On several occasions when Pedro and Enano were entering the POE, United States Inspectors wanted to know if they had met with Olegario. Of course, Pedro and Enano said nothing to the inspectors.

They reported to me they remembered a Hispanic female inspector, wearing a white shirt, dark blue pants, and a badge at the POE, who stopped them when they crossed into the United States. She was very friendly and mentioned her Uncle Olegario. Once again, Pedro and Enano said nothing. She smiled and told the CIs to continue to the United States. Pedro said, "The brothers are proud of their niece working at the Port of Entry."

Pedro said her name was "Anna." At the DEA office, I asked my partner Norman if he knew a woman named Anna Meraz, who worked at the POE. Norman and I met Anna face-to-face at the POE without her knowing who I was. Anna was a charming young lady, nice, not attractive, just short and heavy. Norman remembered Anna and gave her a big hug. I had no idea she was a good friend of his, or that she knew he was DEA. Pedro was right on, and I confirmed she was the same immigration officer who worked at the POE.

I reported to a trusted friend who worked with the INS Office of Personal Responsibility (OPR) about the Meraz niece working at the POE. He said, "I'll check it out."

<><><>

Pedro and Enano met close friends and smugglers of the Meraz brothers in El Golfo. Again, the CIs met with Jose Jonas Rodriguez and Maria Solis-Quesada for the first time.

Maria became a fountain of information, and Pedro developed a sexual relationship with her immediately. Even after he found out, she was one of Oswaldo's girlfriends and a drug smuggler. Maria Solis told Pedro that she drove Olegario and Oswaldo Meraz's narcotics several times from El Golfo to San Luis, Mexico. Oswaldo paid her well. She hated Oswaldo but had sex with him when he demanded it. She liked Pedro, and he took advantage of the situation.

One day when Maria was with Pedro and Enano at Oswaldo's grocery store in Mexico, Pedro asked her how Oswaldo made the easy money from his shrimp business. Maria told them everything about how she smuggled drugs for Oswaldo into the United States from the POE.

She also told him about how Oswaldo was dealing with the Chinese in the shrimp business. Oswaldo didn't make a lot of money selling shrimp. She told Pedro that she could smuggle a kilo of cocaine or a pound of heroin across the POE without any problems from United States inspectors. She asked him, "Do you want me to smuggle a kilo or a pound for you?"

Pedro told me, "Maria is a very attractive woman. After snorting coke, she talked about how the climate in El Golfo is very dangerous, and it isn't safe for Enano and me to go by ourselves. She said the Federales are very bad."

Maria explained to Pedro that the boats would pull up off the coast in El Golfo, Mexico. Oswaldo's small shrimp boats would go out to meet the other boats. On one occasion, an Asian ship gave Oswaldo a lot of shrimp that was ready to move across the POE at the border.

Then she told them about how the girls were placing tin foil bindles inside opened shrimp tails. On one occasion Pedro and Enano accidentally watched Oswaldo's workers cut the shrimp tails open and put small tin foil bindles inside. They knew it was white heroin but couldn't prove it.

They also saw how the girls were sexually abused at Oswaldo's shrimp factory. Pedro was upset. He asked me several times to do something to help the girls. I tried and made some calls to the AUSA office.

I was told to "back off" by my DEA supervisor because, as he put it, "You don't want that kind of relationship with the AUSA office looking into sexually abused children within the Meraz family in Mexico and the United States. Do you understand, Larry?"

Afterward, Pedro told me, "We met Oscar again. He scares me, and so does Jose Jonas."

Nobody outside the DEA office knew that Pedro and Enano were meeting with Oswaldo; only the agents at my office were in on it. During the next several months, the CIs met with Oswaldo about the shrimp business. Oswaldo questioned Pedro, "My brother Oscar tried growing coca plants to produce coca, but it didn't work out. What's the method you use in Colombia to produce coca? Do you think we can grow it here in Mexico?"

Pedro told him, "I don't know the method for growing coca, but maybe I can move it in my shrimp into the U.S."

Oswaldo thought this was funny because it was an idea that hadn't yet been discussed.

Pedro and Enano turned out to be the best CIs I ever worked with. Under my watch, I kept them close. Did I trust them? Heck, no! But there was a lot of law enforcement I didn't trust either.

A few weeks later, Pedro with Enano met with Oswaldo in San Luis. They just talked about the shrimp business. There was no conversation about drugs, just shrimp. Oswaldo and the brothers were very cautious about who they trusted to know about their organization. They were behind several killings including attempted murder of two DEA agents. They had to be careful.

Pedro was excited that these guys were big time, criminals. He wanted to get things rolling.

◇◇◇

Pedro and Enano were paid informants, and therefore protected by me as long they followed directions and didn't violate United States law.

When the name Meraz was mentioned, everybody in Yuma law enforcement knew who they were; the Meraz's had many connections with individual family members and law enforcement.

I traveled to San Luis Rio Colorado, Mexico several times to see the homes of Oswaldo and Olegario. I verified, The CIs and SOIs were right, the Meraz homes were two identical, scaled-down miniatures of the White House. Another house was between them. They called this one the Maquiladora Meraz, known as the Icehouse. It featured an underground tunnel. Pedro and Enano knew I couldn't protect them from the Meraz and the corrupt Mexican cops when they were down in Mexico. I could call the AUSA office, but, it would be a death sentence if someone called Mexico about Pedro and Enano working for DEA.

I was continually watching Olegario's produce trucks and Grande trucks coming across the border at the San Luis POE. If I found trucks carrying drugs, I could seize them, but I wanted a large haul of dope! Things have changed today, of course. You can't seize a vehicle unless you have compelling information that it's carrying contraband or drugs.

The Meraz's were using Grande Manufacturing to launder narcotics proceeds with the help of Enrique Medina-Aguilar. At the time, I received confirmation from the private investigators and my sources that the Grande trucks had drugs hidden inside the furniture. I arranged with Grove Manufacturing that I would not take their trucks, but I would get them to stop transporting drugs by making it very clear the company had to help clean things up.

I was anxious to seize a truck with Meraz dope! As far as I was concerned, it didn't have to be a Grande truck, except that I had good intel that they contained drugs I could find. I was hitting a lot of trucks hard, especially Olegario and Grande trucks. I had them searched inside and out with drug-sniffing dogs. But I found no drugs. I was confused. I had reliable sources working inside the Meraz organization and at Grande Manufacturing in Mexico, providing me information that there were drugs on the trucks.

The Meraz brothers and Grande Manufacturing management knew I was stopping their trucks. Somehow, there was a leak informing the Meraz family. Grande management knew there were problems inside their business.

After I was entrenched in the DEA Yuma office, personnel increased up to four agents. Usually, there were only two agents in the office at one time. My partner was Norman, and sometimes I worked closely with another agent, Jorge. Both Norman and Jorge were good people, and I didn't want to believe either of them was a possible leak in my office. However, they did share information with a suspected corrupt customs agent. They weren't corrupt themselves, but they may have leaked information without being aware the customs agent was sharing it with the Meraz brothers and their close associates.

It was almost like I had the black plague. No one wanted to work with me because of the Meraz's – no one except the private investigators. When the trucks were waiting to cross into the U.S., I asked for help to assist in the searches from a very few selected agents from Border Patrol and the United States Customs who had drug dogs.

Chapter 6: Larry Meets with Jerry Pearce

1991, Larry

I got a call from Jerry Pearce about a case his corporation was working that might connect with mine. I was cautious but excited when he explained how his case involved the Meraz organization using Grove trucks to smuggle drugs into the United States at the San Luis, Arizona border. I'd been thinking about getting some help with this case and what Jerry was saying fit my theories. I listened carefully.

He spoke about the Meraz's and possible corruption. There was a big bell going off in my head! A big cowbell. *I had someone in California who was as interested in the Meraz's as I was.*

Pearce said, "We should meet, but not in Yuma. There's too much corruption in law enforcement down there."

"Yeah, you're right. it's a small town, and too many criminals are connected to corrupt people in law enforcement," I agreed.

"Let's meet at the Old Town Café in San Diego. I'll have two Los Angeles PD narcotics officers with me."

"See you there."

This meeting would be an excellent way to get a feeling about the Pearce Corporation. I did my homework. I didn't work with PIs or sources without checking them out first. In my thinking, you need to know your sources, and you need to know who they are. I checked out Jerry Pearce and his PIs and determined they were good people who knew what they were doing.

I told my group supervisor, "I have a PI working in Los Angeles who wants to talk about the Meraz's. I'm going to meet him in San Diego to find out what he can tell me." I didn't mention corruption at this time. I was still not sure who I could trust or where the leaks might be.

He gave me his okay and then while I was getting things ready to leave for San Diego, I got a call from my boss. He told me he had a meeting with the customs supervisor and mentioned my work with the Meraz case and my meeting to get more information from a private investigator group. I was devastated. Why would he do that? He told me the customs supervisor asked if I could take one of their agents with me because they were also looking at the Meraz's.

I couldn't believe what I was hearing. I had worked so hard to keep a low profile, and now my efforts were for nothing. I asked my boss, "You're telling me I have to take a customs agent with me to San Diego?"

"Yeah, because they're working the case too."

"But they're not working the case with me."

"But Larry, they're working on the Meraz's. This agent is out of Florida, and she doesn't know anything about the Meraz's. She's just going to go with you to see what DEA has already learned."

DEA didn't work well with customs agents and inspectors at the border. We typically didn't share information. The customs supervisor assigned a young female agent to work with me. She had less than a year on the job and no experience working this kind of case. There was nothing wrong with her, but if you're going to give me an agent, provide me with someone with experience. Especially with the severity of what's going on out here.

I had no choice. I accepted my new "partner." We showed up in San Diego. Pearce was walking towards us between two typical-looking narcotics agents. They looked great! One wore baggy shorts and a Bermuda shirt. The other wore blue jeans and an open-collared shirt. They were both smiling as they walked up to us.

Pearce introduced himself and then introduced us to Ray and Chris, the LAPD narcotics guys. I immediately trusted them, and when I'm comfortable with someone, they're part of my family. I take care of family.

"Hi, I'm Larry Hardin."

We shook hands, and Pearce nodded to the girl and asked, "Who's this?"

"She's a customs agent out of Yuma."

"No, I don't want to talk to you, Larry."

"What?"

"I don't want to talk with you." Pearce said, "We're not sharing information with customs," and then turned to walk away.

The two cops grabbed Pearce and convinced him to come back. They told him, "Look, we came down here. Let's go ahead and talk to Larry."

Pearce already knew of corruption inside United States Customs in Yuma. He had done his homework, too. He knew when the Meraz's were involved, and something was taking place. He knew they were using Grande trucks to transport narcotics into the United States, and someone in law enforcement in Yuma was protecting them.

When we sat down and started talking, Pearce kept looking over at Ray and Chris. The next thing I knew, Chris was flirting with the customs agent and said, "Let me buy you ice cream! Come on. Let's go." And she went!

I couldn't believe she would be that naive! You may think he's going to take you out in his car, but who knows what he's going to do to you. I was just happy to have her out of earshot.

Pearce explained to me, "I learned your name from a customs agent in Vegas. He told me, 'Don't deal with customs agents in Yuma. But this Hardin guy seems like he's got good integrity. You may be able to talk to him. He's got an active case going on with all the Meraz's.'"

"Well, Jerry, I'm not here to give you information about what I'm doing but tell me what you have." I had to explain to anyone I was working with that I wasn't able to give them information but could let them know if they were on the right track. I explained this to Pearce, "One thing about my job is that I don't talk about my case with any civilian or private citizen. If you give me information,

I'll check it out. If it's for real, I'll come back and tell you your information is right on. Just be very careful because these are bad people. I'll let you know if it gets too dangerous. If I feel anything is wrong or you're getting too close, I'll tell you."

I listened to what Pearce and Ray knew about the Meraz's and their involvement with Grande Manufacturing in San Luis, Mexico. I didn't offer anything in return.

We talked quite a while about the trucks being used for Meraz criminal activities. We couldn't speak for long, because Chris and the agent came back. After that, Pearce didn't want to talk any more.

I said to Pearce, "I'll tell you what, you come out to Yuma, and I'll meet with you at one of the hotels, and then we can talk about the Meraz's and what you know about corruption."

Driving back from San Diego to Yuma, the girl was crying and said, "I don't like the way they treated me. They wouldn't let me be part of the discussion."

She was intentionally left out of the picture.

"Look, I'm not here to protect you. You're an agent, you have a badge and a gun, and you're assigned to Yuma. You could've stopped that bullshit right away. You're in control. You could have been hard with them up front to calm things down."

She didn't have a handle on the situation and cried all the way to Yuma. I gave her a little education. "You know what, you're a woman, deal with it. You're young and the way you're acting, people will hit on you, especially law enforcement."

Regardless of the drama with the agent, I was impressed with Jerry Pearce. He was very smart and forthright, and I felt like I could trust him, even though he was a PI. He'd been a lieutenant in a Sheriff's Department. I just had a good feeling about him.

<>◇<>

Yuma, AZ

There were a lot of different trucks, including Grove/Grande trucks coming across the border that I knew were being used by the

Meraz's. I just wanted to get one. Pearce told me about Oscar Meraz, who was using the Grande/Grove trucks to smuggle drugs. Oscar was very dangerous, and I warned Pearce to be careful.

In less than two weeks, we set up a meeting in Yuma.

Pearce paged Jeff in Hawthorne and John in Fontana. When they called back, he told them to come to Yuma immediately. Jeff and John drove in that same day and checked into a hotel. Pearce flew his private plane to Yuma to meet them. They were staying at the Shilo Inn, outside of Yuma. It was a very nice hotel for Yuma. I asked DEA agent Norman to go with me because I didn't want to see these private investigators alone. That was something I didn't do.

We all met in Pearce's room. After some discussion, we agreed we had some of the same information on the Meraz organization. The Grove/Grande trucks were still running drugs from Oswaldo Meraz and Raphael Quintero. This was a bad situation. Frank Grover didn't want a scandal involving drugs and have Grove Manufacturing employees look like corporate criminals. Pearce also told me about a lot of law enforcement corruption in Yuma.

I explained, "What you're giving me can really help with my case."

Pearce said, "We're trying to clean this up for Grove Manufacturing. Our clients don't want top managers indicted for something like this. We could sure use your help. My boys will give you information as they get it so we can help each other." He told Jeff and John they would be giving me information and working the case with me.

These were good people who knew what they were doing. They were giving me all the intel.

When we ended the meeting, Norman and I offered to take Jeff and John across the border to see the Meraz homes in Mexico.

<><><>

San Luis, Mexico

The next morning Norman and I met at the office and drove a reddish-brown, beat up, ugly Mercury G-car over to the hotel to pick up Jeff and John. Everything was very professional. "Come on, you two. Come with us." Jeff and John got into the back seat.

Before taking off, Norman popped the trunk, and Jeff said, "What's he doing?" Norman was putting Mexican plates on the vehicle. I told them we do it all the time. We have to, for our safety when doing undercover surveillance in Mexico.

Jeff said, "Wow, I'm getting an education!"

We drove across the border. U.S. Customs knew we were DEA agents, but Mexican Customs didn't. Our back windows were blacked out so no one could see inside the car. John was shooting pictures left and right through the glass. He was an excellent photographer and took advantage of the situation.

I told them, "Okay, we're coming up on it."

"Coming up on what?" Jeff asked.

"On the Meraz homes."

Jeff's mouth dropped. He didn't say anything but told me later, "I was taking it all in and thinking to myself, Wow! They look like two miniature versions of the White House, sitting catty-corner from each other. I can literally see the gun turrets on top of the homes."

I pointed out Olegario's house, right between the other two. "It's called the Congeladora Meraz (Icehouse)."

John was getting lots of pictures to document what we were seeing. I told them, "You need to be very careful. The local cops are protecting the Meraz's. You don't want them to see you taking pictures." It was highly unusual to see homes like that in Mexico. There was no way they would have those homes just from their produce or shrimp businesses.

Chapter 7: Learning More about the Meraz's; *San Luis, AZ*

1992, Randy

Jeff, John, and I spent many hours sitting at the border. Often, we sat in Friendship Park, directly in front of the entrance to the Mexican Port of Entry in San Luis.

One time, John and I were parked, facing east in our rental car, watching vehicles and pedestrians going into Mexico. A guy pulled up and parked about three parking spots away. After a while, it looked like his right shoulder was moving a little, and we couldn't figure out if he was writing something or what he was doing.

I quietly exited the passengers' side of the vehicle and walked behind it, so I could slowly walk up to the passenger side of the other car. When I looked in, I could see the guy was watching the cute Mexican girls going into Mexico. He was jerking off.

Crazy things happened at the border. Anything of value, we would report to Larry. We also had a little fun with him from time to time. I was intrigued by many of the funny things that happened.

◇◇◇

Larry

The private investigators often came back and reminded me of the work they were doing at the border. I knew one day I was going to find drugs on Olegario's produce truck or Oswaldo's shrimp truck. If I could only find the drugs, I could show what the maquiladora was doing. The only explanation was the brothers were getting help from corrupt law enforcement and Meraz relatives at the POE.

The private investigators and I knew the Grande maquiladora business was terrible; working conditions were unpleasant and unsafe. The company used cheap labor. The owners might be Americans, but when they live in the United States and run their business in Mexico, there was something else going on. The Mexican and United States government were making money. I believe, the Meraz's were paying off both sides, and it wasn't the guy getting 50¢ an hour!

I also learned from my sources that the Meraz brothers had other relatives working with Immigration & Naturalization Service (INS) and Customs at the San Luis POE. They informed the Meraz's I was waiting for their trucks to come across from Mexico. There was a leak, and it was dangerous for my sources in Mexico. The leak had to be coming from one of the agents that I trusted, but I wasn't sure which one. Jeff and Randy suspected it was a leak from within my office.

Through hard work, I substantiated that there were approximately 40 traffickers associated with the Meraz brothers, and about 30 of them were related to the family by blood or marriage. The PIs also provided me names of alleged associates who were major Mexican, Southeast Asian, and Colombian traffickers.

I couldn't let anyone in Mexico know which trucks I was going to search, because they would alert their people. But then I noticed something important. I started seeing some trucks drop off their trailers before they arrived at the border. Soon, another truck would pick up the trailer and bring it across. They were switching them up because they assumed they were being targeted. I had the authority from DOJ to seize them, and someone got wind that I was watching.

I was trying to figure out a way to catch members of the Meraz organization, without involving other law enforcement agencies. I also wanted to protect the case from being dismissed by the United States Attorney Office in Phoenix for lack of direct evidence. We only had rumors from former Grande employees that the Meraz's were putting cocaine and heroin into table legs, chair legs, and chair cushions at the plant in Mexico.

Chapter 8: Influence of the Chinese; Torrance, CA

1992

Larry spoke with the AUSA Michael Hope, and later AUSA Richard Dreamer, about the many legal obstacles he had to overcome to avoid such issues as strategies, venue, extradition, and prosecution.

<><><>

Larry

Randy and Jeff gave me information about a Chinese organization in Los Angeles. The next thing I knew, the words "Blue Finn" were popping up from Pedro and other sources about a Chinese organization working with the Meraz brothers in San Luis, Mexico. Pedro told me when he met with Oswaldo; he was talking about deliveries of shrimp they were preparing and shipping to Blue Finn Seafood Company in Los Angeles and Phoenix. I didn't see the connection. With those living in the Los Angeles area connected to the Blue Finn Seafood Company, this was a higher level of trafficking.

I thought to myself; This is unheard of! Throughout my whole career, I had never heard of the Chinese and Mexicans working together to move drugs into the United States. When the Chinese do white heroin, they deal strictly with their own group of people. But for them to get involved with the Mexicans? Something is going on out there from the top, allowing these Chinese people to mix in with the Meraz cartel, right there in Meraz country. It takes someone higher up to make those kinds of connections. You've got to have the Chinese and Mexican governments working together to make something like that happen!

I was getting more excited and if I'm honest, a bit nervous. It was overwhelming. I was just one agent. The Asian connections were way beyond me!

There was a DEA task force of agents in Los Angeles targeting Chinese drug activities. Randy mentioned a DEA agent, Sam Little working with the Asian Task Force in Los Angeles.

In February 1988, three DEA agents, George Montoya, 37, Paul Seema, 52, and Jose Martinez, 25, working as undercover members of the Asian Gang Task Force in Los Angeles were ambushed in Pasadena while purchasing $80,000 worth of heroin from Asian drug dealers. Montoya and Seema were killed, and Martinez was severely injured. Backup DEA agents killed two of the Asian gang members and a third man, Win Wei Wang, also known as William Wang, 18, was shot eight times when pursued by agents after the ambush. Su Te Chia, also known as Michael Chia, 21, was involved in planning the murders. Wang and Chia were indicted in 1988 for two counts of murder and one count each of attempted murder, robbery, and conspiracy to rob federal agents.[62]

At the time, United States Attorney Robert Bonner wanted Wang and Chia to face the death penalty. "It's lamentable. Indeed, it is astonishing that it is not possible to obtain the death penalty under federal law for the murder of federal agents. ... Only Congress can remedy this glaring inadequacy in the federal law"[63] Chia's case was overturned in 2004 because Wang stated Chia was not part of the shooting.[64, 65, 66]

<><><>

I told Pedro to focus on whether the connection between Oswaldo's shrimp business and Blue Finn Seafood Company was real and not false information.

I called DEA Sam Little, case agent in Los Angeles. Sam knew the Pearce Corporation were focused on Blue Finn Seafood Company and Asian activities with the Meraz brothers. Sam and I had worked together with intelligence on a previous case. I would describe him as lazy when it came to prosecution. He never made a case where he put someone in jail. He was more of a problem than anything else and was of no help to me.

<><><>

Jeff

Sam explained to John and me about the Blue Finn Seafood Company that began many years earlier. The company was started in 1974, after the Vietnam War, by three brothers: Lan Bao Yang, Mu Xun Yang, and Shan Shui Yang. They were previously certified triads (Chinese Cartels) in China. The Blue Finn Seafood Company grew enormously over a short period. One brother was a dentist, and one ran a restaurant. They had no experience in running an operation like the Blue Finn Seafood Company.

After hearing Sam Little's information, John and I believed the United States government financed the Yang brothers through the CIA to open the Blue Finn Seafood Company. The theory was the sole function of Blue Finn Seafood Company was laundering money and drugs for CIA operations. I thought, *Little was paid to keep eyes off the Blue Finn Seafood Company. It was like DEA protecting Blue Finn Seafood Company, maybe on behalf of the CIA? Even so, the Blue Finn Seafood Company appeared clean as a whistle.*

The CIA put in an operative, Hugo Salazar, to watch the three Chinese brothers. He was the go-between for CIA, working for the Blue Finn Seafood Company and a government employee.

James Lawrence had previously been interested in Blue Finn Seafood Company, but he didn't have a clue of the dynamics of the company or anything else connected to it. He closed the case because he couldn't prove there were drugs connected to Grove Manufacturing.

<><><>

Randy

John and I tailed Hugo Salazar and the Yang brothers. We had the name, Meraz, and were now given the task of finding out who they were and who related to the Grove case and the trucks making deliveries to the Blue Finn Seafood Company.

Through delicate research, I discovered that Lan Yang's house was government property, tax-exempt. He lived in Rancho Palos Verdes, on the peninsula. I learned this when I went to the Los Angeles County Assessor's Office, downtown to check into Lan Yang's property. On the microfiche, it said, "Tax-exempt." When I went back a week later to double-check, this time, it didn't say "Tax-exempt." So, I asked the girl at the counter about the change.

She said, "Well, let me go in the back and see if I can figure something out."

About five minutes later, she came back and said, "I found this card catalog thing that holds microfiche in the back. I think this might have what you're looking for. Just come on back."

I went in the back and looked for it on the microfiche. It was one of those old machines you must scroll through until you find the information you're looking for. It took a while to see it on the screen. When I found the property again, I was surprised to find it said, "Tax-exempt." There it was! The one I found in the public files did not say it. I was smart enough to photocopy it this time.

I left the assessor's office with a photocopy of the property information and was thinking: "How do some of these guys get tax-exempt property?"

When I reported back to Pearce and Frank Grover at our next meeting, they immediately told me, "We need to dig further into that."

When John and I went back to the assessor's office a month later, we found the same thing I'd seen the last time in the public files. It did not say "Tax-exempt." I walked up to the desk and the same lady I talked to before was there. I asked her if I could look at the one, she showed me the last time in the back.

She said, "No, I got in so much trouble for showing you that. Apparently, that box is not for public viewing." She's not supposed to show anything non-public to the public.

I was thinking: This is typical for a cover-up. There are many reasons why they would have tax-exempt property. They could be Defense Contractors where the company works for the government in some capacity. However, it's usually not hidden from public view. In almost the "worst-case" scenario in those situations, there would at least be a note in the file for the public stating, "This particular record is not for public display." Never is there a fake record made to appear the owner pays taxes.

This led John and I to conclude that this may be connected to U.S. Intelligence operations covering up for this guy. Ordinarily that would not be my first thought, however, more information was coming to my attention about intelligence operators involved. We reported everything to Frank Grover, and it was left for him to decide what it meant.

Dianne DeMille PhD, Larry Hardin, Jeffrey Pearce, Randy Torgerson

Chapter 9: Jeff in Yuma and Larry's Sample Buys; *Yuma & San Luis, AZ*

1993, Jeff

When I flew in on Mondays, I would drive into town and check into one of the hotels. I would pick up my rental car and my radio. In those days, we used what was called a microwave system. It wasn't as secure as our current cellular system. Nothing was secure about communications between Mexico and the United States at the border.

My daily routine started with meeting and receiving information from my CI. I did surveillance at the port of entry, or the truck yard where the Grande trucks would come in from Mexico and the Grove trucks would take the loads to delivery locations in California and Arkansas.

Erik and I would often conduct long surveillances that started in Arizona and ended up in Texas. There was a time when I went undercover as a freelance journalist to get information from potential suspects. Sometimes I could be relentless in getting the information I wanted.

Erik and I became friends with Larry. During the first year, we began to develop a camaraderie working together. He taught us a lot about working narcotics and being undercover.

When we gave Enrique F. Medina's name to Larry, he got very excited. He knew we were on the same path as his CIs, Pedro, and Enano.

One CI I developed, Fernando Lopez, was a fellow serviceman and an extremely well-decorated Vietnam war hero. I connected with Fernando after he got out of the service. He was a commissioned officer who took multiple snipers rounds to the stomach. He had a difficult time with his wounds from Vietnam.

He was working as a driver for Grove Manufacturing with shipments of heroin and cocaine offloaded at Blue Finn Seafood Company. We interviewed Fernando, and he became a long-term confidential informant (CI). His info was primarily good. He was an excellent CI for me. Fernando smoked marijuana with the Meraz's and enlightened us on some things he knew about them. I found him to be a good informant for what I needed. He didn't know everything about them, which diminished his role as a CI for Larry.

When Larry heard the name Fernando Lopez, he looked into the military archives. He called the archives department and gave the information we had on Fernando. He found out Fernando was a war hero. He'd been a poor Mexican from Texas who got into some trouble with local law enforcement. The judge offered him prison or Vietnam. He chose Vietnam and was battlefield-enlisted. He then moved up to officer. Fernando took two rounds in Vietnam while trying to find a sniper. Larry met him when he was undercover with Pearce. Fernando told me he thought Larry was CIA. He had no clue he was DEA.

At one point, we had Fernando purchase a small amount of heroin directly from Enrique. Jeff gave him a small recorder that could tape one side and continue recording on side two without having to remove and flip the cassette over. This was cool technology in the 1990s. He was easily able to conceal it when he met with Enrique.

Fernando purchased black tar heroin and recorded the transaction with Enrique in Spanish. When they called me, they described how it went down. I came over and field-tested the heroin right there. It was almost 100% pure. I took a statement from Fernando and took the tape and the heroin and into custody. Fernando still thought Larry was CIA!

Fernando didn't have the level to buy directly from the Meraz's, but he could buy from Enrique. And Enrique was integral to the case and the introduction to the Meraz's. He was at a lot of the meetings that took place with the Meraz's and CIs. Fernando didn't know Pedro and Enano before their meeting with the Meraz's.

◇◇◇

San Luis, AZ
Larry

Enrique and Fernando were present, along with Pedro and Enano, during one of the Oompa parties (Mexican parties with Mexican bands) at the Meraz mansions. Olegario boasted, "DEA will never be able to touch me because of my connection with CIA and what I've done for them. They come to me for information. So, I'm pretty much protected."

Now maybe I can get someone inside Grande in Mexico to get more information I need. According to an eyewitness and sources, Congeladora Meraz was where they brought fish and shrimp loads from the barquitos, fishing boats, where they picked up the heroin in El Golfo. The heroin was from a Chinese ship off the coast. They took the drugs and shrimp to the Icehouse. These were size-ten jumbo shrimp. Huge tiger shrimp! Big enough to hide drugs in a cavity cut under the tail.

I met with Pedro and Enano when they came across the border at a neutral location off-site.

I told the men, "Start talking about computer chips [slang for drugs] in your shrimp trucks, anything that can make extra money. The brothers know you're Colombian and Colombia is known for cocaine, heroin, and marijuana. Throw it out there again that you're interested in getting some extra money, but your shrimp business is failing. Just mention it casually."

It took time for Pedro and Enano to earn Oswaldo's trust, and time to get the "big fish." I had the time to give Don and Roy justice.

Pedro and Enano met with Enrique's brother-in-law at a grocery store near the United States border in San Luis, Mexico. Now I was thinking: *Why did Pedro go to a grocery store? Why a grocery store?*

Pedro started purchasing from Oscar small samples of heroin and chemicals to make meth. He was attempting to obtain from

Olegario 30 kilos of coke for $14,500 a kilo. I asked FBI Mark Spencer again, "Will you help me buy 30 kilos?"

Spencer said nothing because he needed to talk to his boss. Later, Spencer told me he no longer wanted to be involved with the Meraz case, and he never gave me a reason why.

Pedro and Enano were making connections for a conspiracy case against the brothers. I was getting factual evidence for the AUSA office to prosecute the brothers, and I was getting excited again. *This is what I've been working towards. Everything's taking shape here!* Don and Roy, I'm going to get the brothers!

If I could take the drug traffickers at the Grande company level and connect them directly to the Meraz brothers, then I could develop the link analysis. There was a vast pool of informants we needed to develop. Informants could be in the Los Angeles area, where the Grove and Oswaldo trucks were headed, and in Mexico. Because my informants and I were a bunch of white guys, there was no question about it; we needed some Mexican CIs or sources to help me. I already had Pedro and Enano but still required a Mexican CI.

Chapter 10: Gathering More Information; Yuma, AZ

1992, Larry

I met with Jeff, Erik, and Randy regularly as they got further into the case. I felt very comfortable with them like we were all on the same page and would keep this case close-knit. They gave me names and information on Grande employees and how the Meraz brothers might be using the trucks to smuggle drugs into the states.

They gave me the name of the manager at Grande, Enrique Medina. I couldn't tell them anything. After listening, I just said, "Your name is a hit. It is narcotics-related."

I was thinking: "I have everything I need on this Medina guy. Enrique is the brother-in-law to the Meraz brothers. I'm trying to find a weak link into the Meraz family. Women and money are the downfall of any culture. I discovered this was Enrique's weakness."

Jeff and Randy assumed Enrique of Grove/Grande Manufacturing was the manager and had to be a part of the illegal activities. There was a fair amount of it going on at Grande that was later validated.

Randy and John got Grove/Grande employee names, managers names, and more. They did background checks on most, especially those in Mexico. Some of the managers of the maquiladora company, working Mexicans, lived in the United States or at least had a house there. Manager Aldo Campo was one of those guys.

They started to figure out who at Grande was involved with Enrique and whether they were part of the actual Meraz organization. Or, *was it like with the mob, as Jeff described it, where you're the "made" guy, you're in with the mob, but you're not family, you're not blood. But you're "made," meaning you work for them and are protected by them.* There were a lot of employees of Grove/Grande Manufacturing who knew the

Meraz's. The main ones were in the cartel and were Meraz organization members: brothers, cousins, or a "made" guy.

<><><>

In 1995 I was sitting in my office reading, leaning back in my chair with my feet up on the desk. I got a call: "Hi, this is Robert Bonner. I represent Grove Manufacturing. I understand you're targeting the Grande trucks coming across the Mexican border."

I was startled. The name was familiar, and I asked, "Who are you, now?" I don't like lawyers, even when they're on my side. They tend to lie a lot and can be brutal. It's a game with these lawyers.

"My name is Robert Bonner."

"Do you work for DEA?"

"Yes, I'm a former DEA administrator."

My feet hit the floor! "Sir, why are you calling me?"

Bonner stated in a soft voice, "I'm representing Grande, and I'd like to come out and meet with you."

Bonner was my DEA administrator a few years ago. He was well-known and well-liked by everyone in the DEA.

We agreed to meet at a hotel in Yuma. I advised my supervisor about the meeting. He immediately called DEA central office in Phoenix.

My boss got back to me and said, "No, you're not going to meet with Mr. Bonner in Yuma. Instead, you'll meet with him at the DEA office in Phoenix, Arizona."

I tried to explain that Bonner didn't want to go to Phoenix to be around all that DEA hoopla. He wanted to focus on my investigation. My boss refused to let me meet Bonner in Yuma.

When I arrived at the DEA office in Phoenix, there were two other guys in the elevator with me. I didn't know who they were or why they were going to the same office. They looked at me, I looked at them, and I knew there was going to be a problem. I had the feeling the CIA knew I was focusing on the Blue Finn Seafood

Company and the Meraz's. Once off the elevator, I asked the secretary who the guys were.

"CIA from Los Angeles," she said.

Why is CIA meeting with my "big bosses? Maybe they're friends of Bonner's? Or were they here for something else?

Phoenix management had control of the meeting, so when Mr. Bonner and I finally met in the Phoenix office, we weren't able to talk about the case. Instead, we made small talk. Later, Mr. Bonner went outside the office to smoke in the parking lot. I was standing there outside, alone, thinking about the two CIA agents. Mr. Bonner was disappointed because we didn't have a chance to talk about the Grande investigation. The only thing he said to me outside in the parking lot was, "We will talk again."

"Yes, sir!"

I gave Mr. Bonner my respect. Even though he was a private attorney, he was my former DEA administrator. I eventually got to know him through the case.

I met Mr. Bonner again with Jerry Pearce at the United States Attorney's office in Phoenix. Mr. Bonner came there to try to convince United States Attorney Janet Napolitano and her staff that I had a good case, and Napolitano's office should prosecute the Meraz brothers. Ms. Napolitano was not present at the meeting. She let her attorneys run the meeting.

The way Napolitano's United States Attorneys sat there and treated Pearce and Bonner at the meeting was terrible. The attorneys were so rude, telling the men and me there wasn't enough evidence to present to a Federal Grand Jury. *Strange, I had enough evidence on the Meraz that the Yuma County attorneys were ready to indict the brothers.*

Phoenix management had control of the meeting, so when Mr. Bonner and I finally met in the Phoenix office, we weren't able to talk about the case

A lot of people were involved here. It wasn't just about the Meraz's. It was also about the Chinese. And it was becoming very personal to me. Same with Jeff, Randy, Erik, and John. It's just the way it was in this business. I was working other cases at the same time and could have let this one go, but how could I after the relationships I'd built with the private investigators? They were giving me all kinds of information and intel to support my case, and we were becoming close friends.

I was distraught because Bonner was my former Administrator, and Pearce was a former Sheriff Lieutenant. They both came from good backgrounds in law enforcement and deserved some respect. Bonner, Pearce, and I knew the Meraz case was ready to be presented to a grand jury. Don and Roy deserved to have a grand jury review the evidence we gathered.

Chapter 11: Watching Deliveries; Los Angeles, CA

1993, Randy

For about three to four months, I did surveillance in South Central, Los Angeles.[67] A lot was happening there. Mexican Grove Manufacturing employees were bringing drugs up to Los Angeles. They would make deliveries to some of the homes in South Central. Some of these homes were located where black gangs lived and congregated. Then they'd go to homes of the Mexicans.

When I first saw this happening, I thought, *There's about to be a shoot-out between Black and Mexican gangs.* I tried to find a pay phone where I knew I could page LAPD and receive calls.

As it turned out, the two gangs were working with each other. And they also had the Chinese bringing in white heroin. They delivered to some of the same homes.

The Pearce Corporation discovered the Chinese were bringing the heroin from the area of El Golfo, Mexico, where Oswaldo Meraz had his shrimp business and a grocery store. We knew it was coming into the U.S. hidden in seafood, primarily in shrimp tails. When they were off duty, Grove truck drivers would drive other trucks, usually box trucks from Mexico with drugs in them. They delivered seafood, mainly jumbo shrimp. Sometimes they drove semis that may not have been Grove trucks.

We started to tie the Chinese to the Mexicans and blacks. We discovered there were several covert meetings between the Yangs and the Mexican cartel in Los Angeles. We also determined that some Mexican government officials would meet on Chinese ships anchored 20-50 miles off the coast. That was a great place to have meetings because no one could surveil them there.

Back in the '70s when crack cocaine came to Los Angeles, local dealers received deliveries from Grove Manufacturing employees on their trucks and Blue Finn Seafood Company's shrimp trucks. Grove trucks were taking drugs into homes in South Central LA.

Most of the cocaine and later manufactured into crack cocaine, was coming from the Mexican Cartels. It was coming across the POEs at the Mexican border. It came into California through San Luis, Calexico, CA, Tijuana, Tecate, or Otay Mesa POEs. The Meraz Organization controlled San Luis, Sonora, Mexico POE, and a relative controlled Calexico, CA POE.[68]

Gary Webb, a reporter with San Jose Mercury News, began writing articles in 1996 about crack cocaine in the Los Angeles area. Shortly after he wrote a couple of pieces, I got a call from Webb asking me, "What do you know about the interactions of Mexicans working with Asians and blacks in South Central Los Angeles?"[69]

I talked to him several times and gave him some information he could use. He got information from many sources, and my information helped tie things together for his story.

A court case involving a local drug dealer claimed that the CIA was behind the dealing of cocaine with the blacks in the area. During the dealer's arraignment, the dealer's girlfriend reached out to Webb, and said, "You need to come to hear this arraignment. He's pleading not guilty, and the government wants him to take a plea bargain because they don't want anything to come out."[70]

Webb asked her, "What do you mean? He's dealing drugs, and the government is behind it?"

The dealer had the attitude, "You can't mess with me because the government is behind this!" That only enticed Webb to continue to tell the story.

Gary Webb published a three-part series in 1996 about the investigation he worked on for over a year. He won a Pulitzer Prize and stunned the world with his series about, "The roots of the crack cocaine epidemic in America, specifically in Los Angeles. The series, titled 'Dark Alliance,' revealed that for the better part of a decade, a Bay Area drug ring sold tons of cocaine to Los Angeles street gangs and funneled millions in drug profits to the CIA-backed Nicaraguan Contras."[71]

82

He wrote about how "our government knowingly allowed massive amounts of drugs and money to change hands at the expense of our communities."[72] The series "documented a network of collusion in the 1980s that joined together the crack cocaine explosion, the Contras, and the CIA."[73]

He stated on the Montel Williams show in 1996 that cocaine was being delivered to South Central Los Angeles, San Francisco, San Jose, and Oakland throughout the 1980s.[74]

Webb had been warned not to pursue his concerns with the CIA. A former journalist was fired when he began a similar story. For a while, the story was big news. However, after a few months, newspapers started to discredit his report and knocked down his credibility. They debunked the claim that "The CIA deliberately unleashed the crack epidemic on black America."[75]

The actual message Webb was trying to convey was lost with the controversy surrounding media claims. He had made several substantive points about CIA doing business with Nicaragua and bringing drugs into the U.S. in exchange for arms.[76] Later, CIA and other agencies conducted investigations into claims Webb made in his series that also discredited his report.

"Two years later, the CIA's internal investigation proved to be a vindication of Gary Webb's work. So would another internal investigation conducted by the Justice Department."[77] Gary wrote, "It wasn't so much a conspiracy that I had outlined as it was a chain reaction."[78]

The CIA internal investigation acknowledged "that the agency had covered up Contra drug trafficking for more than a decade…which confirmed key chunks of Webb's allegations."[79] "The CIA's inspector general later corroborated Webb's key findings, but by then, his career was wrecked."[80]

Webb was destroyed by the accusations and investigations surrounding his information. He wrote the series into a book, *Dark Alliance* and later, *Dark Alliance: The CIA, the Contras, and the Crack Cocaine Explosion*.[81] His life was turned upside-down, and on December 10, 2004, Webb reportedly committed suicide at age 49.

There was a movie about Gary Webb's story, 2014's *Kill the Messenger*, and there are several YouTube interviews with him that are available to view. Another person, former DEA Undercover Agent Mike Levine, wrote several books about corruption, drugs, and the cartels that parallel many of Webb's stories. Among his books are *The Big White Lie* and *Double Crossed*. There are several YouTube interviews – one includes both Levine and Webb on the Montel Williams show from 1996.[82, 83]

Chapter 12: Randy in Marina del Rey; *El Centro & San Onofre, CA*

1996

John and I did some surveillance in El Centro, California. We wanted to see if trucks going to South Central L.A. were the same trucks coming from Grande Manufacturing. Almost weekly, our informants gave us anonymous tips about drugs coming across on Grande/Grove trucks. We followed the trucks coming up Highway 8, connecting to Highway 5, and continuing to Los Angeles. There's a checkpoint at San Onofre, and when we got the word, usually late at night that there were drugs on one of the trucks, we would drive down and follow it. Since the trucks were required to stop at the scales, this was an excellent place to observe what was happening. Many times, I got the call, and I would call Ray Shorb, who was part of the task force. We would head down to San Onofre, about a one-hour drive down the coast from Marina del Rey. We rarely found anything. Often, John would go with us.

On Monday, early in the morning, John and I got a call about a truck with drugs coming into San Onofre. We were in Fresno and went straight to the rental car place, picked up our car, and headed for San Onofre. We hadn't eaten lunch yet, so we stopped at a gas station in Delano and bought two brown bag sandwiches. John was driving, and I was in the passenger seat, eating my lunch.

All of a sudden, John looked at me and pulled over. He said, "Shit! Are you okay? Are you okay?"

I just looked at him. "Why? What's wrong with you?"

"Look in the mirror."

I flipped the visor down, "Holy shit! What's going on? There must be something bad in this sandwich. Maybe I'm allergic to something."

My neck and head were red and swollen. Not only swollen, but I had hives all over my body.

John said, "Should we drive back to Fresno or go to the hospital?"

We had just left Delano and were about a half-hour from Bakersfield. There was nothing around.

This was going to cause us to lose time, and we needed to get to San Onofre.

"Let's just continue to Bakersfield. We can stop at the next gas station. Maybe I can get some Benadryl. That's probably all the doctor would do. If that doesn't help, then we can go back home."

We saw a gas station and stopped. I bought some Benadryl and took it right away. Things started to calm down by the time we got to Bakersfield. We decided to keep going, and in another couple of hours, we arrived in San Onofre. By then, I was fine, and I was so relieved.

We could see the customs agents checking the trucks coming across the border. Agents had their dogs to alert them when a vehicle had drugs aboard. Sometimes they had useful information, but if the dogs didn't alert, the truck couldn't be searched. The dogs had the authority to search. Unless they wanted to disclose who the informant was. Which they did not do.

About 95% of the time, if anything was found, it was just a smidgen of black tar heroin or a little bit of marijuana, only a usable amount. Nothing else! The dogs would alert. We used a few informants, not just one. Some knew each other; some didn't. There was just no way they could all be wrong all the time. Our informants couldn't all be playing us. We expected that to happen with some, but not all of them!

We received tips of drugs on Grove trucks, but that wasn't enough to start pulling anything out of them. We'd have to unload the whole truck. We thought if they didn't have the dogs, there was probably be another way we could find the drugs.

Years later, we discovered why these trucks were not stopped. In the early 2000s, a couple of border patrol agents who were dog handlers working at the checkpoint retrained their dogs to

86

only alert when they wanted the dogs to. They had been paid off by the cartel and eventually arrested.[84]

We had to reevaluate. Why are our informants telling us a truck has drugs when it was a different truck carrying the drugs? We shifted our view so we could see the line of vehicles as they came across the border.

We could see young kids walking between cars and spraying them from a water bottle. The drivers didn't pay attention. The kids would spray one car or truck and then skip a couple and spray the next one. If somebody said something, the kids would ask, "Can I wash your windows?"

Usually, the person would answer, "No, I don't want you to wash my windows." But the kid would spray anyway and walk away.

The marijuana spray drove the dope dogs crazy. We determined that someone south of the border was having this done intentionally. Not necessarily to get around border patrol but to distract their dogs and keep the customs agents occupied, so they let some vehicles through without searching them.

Later, we found out the Meraz organization employed kids to spray lots of vehicles with a mixture of marijuana and water before entering the U.S. from Mexico. As they approached the border, the kids sprayed marijuana underneath the trailer of 18-wheeler trucks and the tires.

Some Border Patrol agents and Immigration officers had family in Mexico who worked for the drug cartels. The agents and officers made extra income by alerting (or not alerting) the drug traffickers when the trucks came across.

We also learned later that some uniformed officers, mainly highway patrol, picked up drugs across the border and then transported it to San Francisco and other northern regions. Who's going to pull over a highway patrol car?

Even though we found these things out years after the case was over, it was still nice to know we weren't crazy! When we were investigating the case, our informants were largely not lying to us. The drugs were certainly there. We just couldn't find them.

Chapter 13: Experiences on the Job; *San Diego, CA*

1994, Randy

A couple of months later, I followed a lead going into San Diego that took me up into the mountains. I was about five miles from the border of Mexico. I went to the end of the road, got out, and walked to the top of the hill where there was a hiking path going down the other side. Down below on the other side of the hill, I could see a valley. I went back to my car and got the binoculars. I could see a dirt trail that went to a small ranch below. There were lots of chickens and two parallel dirt paths with grass in the middle that went from the chicken ranch to a small clump of trees further down. Everything was all bare except for a cluster of trees in the middle. I had to move closer to see what was in the clump of trees.

There were approximately 10-15 good-sized trees clumped together. In the middle of the trees, I could see a huge rock, a boulder, that was about two feet shorter than the trees. On the boulder was painted a big red X. The first thing I thought was, *This is just like in the movies. It's an "airdrop!"* I reported it to Larry, and as usual, he entered it into his computer system.

About a week later, I was driving around Los Angeles and got a page from my office. I called the office, and the secretary told me, "You had a call from San Diego. It was from an informant who wants to talk to you about some information he has for you."

At the time, I didn't have any informants in San Diego who would have my office number. I had to find a pay phone where I could receive a call because I only had a pager number.

I was in Hawthorne and remembered a bowling alley nearby with a pay phone where I could make a call. I drove to the bowling alley and paged the guy. A minute later, the phone rang. I answered, "Hello, someone called my office and left this pager number."

"Are you Randy?"

Cautiously, I responded, "Yeah."

"Ok, well, thanks for calling me."

"No problem. Who are you?"

The guy was pleasant but didn't really give me any information. He wanted to know about the chicken ranch I had seen. I assumed he was in law enforcement or something like that, but I couldn't get him to say so. I was sure the guy was Caucasian because he didn't have any accent.

This guy was asking a lot of questions and not telling me anything about who he was. I told him, "You're asking me a lot of questions. If we meet in person, and you identify yourself, I'll be more than happy to tell you what I know."

He finally told me he was with the Department of Justice.

"Ok, that's fabulous! However, you still need to meet me in person and show me your identification. Then I'll tell you anything and everything."

The conversation continued as we went around in circles for about five to ten minutes. Things got heated up to where the guy on the other end started to demand I tell him what he wanted to know.

"I can't be more clear. I'm happy to tell you what you want to know as long as you're in law enforcement of some kind and show me your identification."

After he realized he wasn't getting anything from me, he yelled, "You're in over your head. You don't know what the fuck you're doing! Shit happens to people!"

He was making me mad at that point and continued, "You have no idea who you're dealing with!" I thought he meant something about the cartel.

"You little fucker, you don't know who you're dealing with! Or who I know," and I hung up on him.

As I got in my car, I thought to myself, *Wow, he just threatened me*!

I called Ray Shorb, LAPD Major Division, who worked with the guys in Los Angeles dealing with drug cases, ten kilos and above. I got very close to Ray over the years, not only with this case but with a couple of previous cases. He was almost like a father figure to me. I told him what happened.

Ray got mad and said, "Give me that pager number!"

An hour later he called me back and said, "He's a DEA agent out of El Centro. I called him, and we got into a pissing match. My captain called his captain, and we're all going to meet. I'll get back to you on this."

Ray and his captain went quickly to meet this guy in San Diego with his captain. They came back and said everything seemed legit, but I could tell they weren't sure.

I told them, "Look, Larry went into the computer, but this guy didn't go into the DEA computer to get my information because my office number wouldn't be in those records. I don't give it out to many people. So where did he get it?" It was a mystery.

From Ray's perspective, this guy had a lead, and he was trying to get information from me. I figured he's either working with CIA or the cartel!

At the end of the day, the guy was ordered to call and apologize. He paged me a day or so later, in the evening. I used the phone on the boat to return his page. The guy said to me, "I apologize, I didn't know who you knew, and I shouldn't have spoken to you the way I did."

In hindsight, I should have asked more questions. I probably wouldn't have got any more information. This guy got caught. I still wasn't sure how he got my name to come up with a lead. I don't deal with drugs. He didn't have any legitimate drug source telling him to tell me. Somehow, he must have scanned the information I reported to Larry. That's the only thing way I could think of where he would get my information.

I'd been out in the middle of nowhere. It's possible someone may have been hiding in the bushes, as a lookout, or they could have run the rental car license plates. I don't know how else he got my number. Or a criminal gave it to him.

<><><>

El Centro, CA

Another time, Jeff and I had an informant who told us about a smaller truck loaded with 5,000 pounds of cocaine. We didn't know how true it was, but we reported it to Larry.

Larry got his Customs Task Force to do surveillance and border patrol. The truck came across in El Centro, California. Six cars were surveilling the truck to see who was expecting a delivery. The agents following the truck had to alert other law enforcement of their progress. They couldn't keep it a secret because that would cause more problems.

Jeff and I were listening in on the radio dispatch but were not part of the surveillance. We wanted to hear what was happening. The truck came across the border, and John and I heard, "We've got eyes on it," "Okay, we're following him now."

About 15 minutes into the surveillance, we heard, "I lost it," and "I lost the vehicle!" We were out in the country. There were no traffic situations to worry about. How could you lose a truck? It's just an old rickety truck that couldn't go much more than 50 mph. This situation helped convinced us that this must be connected to Grove Manufacturing.

About 45 minutes later, a Riverside County Sherriff said, "Hey, I found that truck! I'm behind it now."

We were sure customs and border patrol agents were saying to each other, "Oh, shoot! Now, what are we going to do?"

The sheriff pulled the truck over and arrested the driver.

<><><>

Jeff

Jeffrey & Randy
Working Together

I was thinking: *Okay, this will be a great interrogation!* And was trying to get the proper law enforcement guys on the case to go together to Riverside County Sherriff's office with him. The next morning, before we got everything arranged, the driver was released, and no one seemed to know what happened to the truck. I had one of the officers at the station check on what was entered into the system. It just said the driver was released in the "Furtherance of Justice."

That meant he was an informant and would be providing bigger information than the crime he committed. That was the only way law enforcement would cut someone a break. Because they were planning to get information on something even bigger. I was thinking: *What's he got that's going to be bigger than two tons of cocaine?* The truck disappeared, and no one knew where the driver went or what really happened.

<><><>

Randy

There was one load of shrimp that went from Oswaldo in San Luis, Mexico, directly to Blue Finn Seafood Company in Los Angeles. It was stopped in Phoenix. Jeff, Erik, and I were following when we caught up to the truck. We saw a pile of shrimp, broken, and thrown away in the dumpster.

I commented to Jeff and Erik, "Why, would you destroy thousands of dollars' worth of shrimp? Why would you do that? The logical answer was they were taking the bundles of cocaine out and leaving the shrimp behind."

Dianne DeMille PhD, Larry Hardin, Jeffrey Pearce, Randy Torgerson

Chapter 14: More Experiences on the Job; *Las Vegas, NV*

1992-1996, Jeff

Law enforcement, including some DEA agents and some Yuma PD, couldn't stand us. We were a thorn in their side because we couldn't be controlled. Law enforcement officers and agents couldn't figure out how we had so much valid information about the Meraz's. But Larry protected us.

Larry already had the case going in Yuma, and the information we were providing him was really picking up. He developed a trust with us, and we developed a trust with him. He heard from Pearce about how we protected and supported each other.

At one point, Erik and I were working with the microwave system. We listened to several phone calls, and a couple of them were about a truck transporting cargo from a plant in San Luis, Mexico, to a company in Las Vegas, Nevada. The owner of the gaming company in Las Vegas said he overheard some of their cargo was stolen from his trucks on the way to Nevada.

Erik and I recognized the voice whenever he made a call. The company owner's voice was one you could identify out of a million. One day we heard him say he was meeting with someone at a Chinese restaurant in Yuma, the Mandarin Palace.

So, I said to Erik, "We may be able to pick up some work for Jerry or us. Let's go over to the Mandarin Palace and find a way to make an introduction to this guy."

We went to dinner at the Mandarin Palace and watched for the owner of the gaming company to come in. We didn't know what he looked like, but his voice was unmistakable. When the guy walked in, I said, "This guy looks like an old Jewish mobster. It's got to be him."

As soon as he opened his mouth, we recognized his voice immediately and knew it was him. Erik and I were sitting one table away, thinking about how to approach him.

He was a big guy, enormous. When he got up out of his seat, his money clip fell out of his pants as he walked toward the front.

I picked it up; I'm guessing he had about $5,000 in cash!

I walked up and handed it over as I said, "Sir, I think you dropped this."

"You know, most people would have kept the money. You're an honest young man," he said.

We started talking. I told him I was a private investigator and said, "If you ever need anything, give me a call, and I'll try and help you."

That's when he opened up and said, "Actually, I do have an issue." He went on to tell me about his trucks going to Las Vegas where blank casino chips were being stolen before they got to his company. His company prints chips for different casinos in Vegas. They weren't worth anything. He wanted help to find out who was stealing them before they got to his location.

Pearce Corporation started working on the case. Erik and I watched trucks for Grove/Grande, as well as those involved with the gaming company in Las Vegas. We brought on Larry Mosser, a retired Las Vegas PD officer to work undercover in Las Vegas on the casino case. I knew Larry because I had worked with him on an earlier case.

We were able to find two guys who were stealing the blank chips from the trucks and detailing them with the logos and markings for one of the casinos. They were perfect counterfeit chips, and they were able to use them at the casino as cash for their gambling. The casino had no clue these were counterfeit until we got involved and pointed out a small discrepancy in the printing. This was a quick case, and Larry Mosser helped us identify the chips and led us to the two guys who were making them. The guys were prosecuted six months later by the Las Vegas District Attorney.

<><><>

San Luis, AZ

After the casino chips case was solved, John and Erik wanted to work together more than they had. So, Jerry sent them to Los Angeles on a couple of projects. Since Larry Mosser was still on the payroll doing some work with Randy, Jerry sent him to work with me on the Meraz/Grove case for about six months.

Erik and I observed Grove trucks from the border going into Rodriguez Tire Shop right after crossing the border at San Luis. Jose Rodriguez's family were the owners but lived in Colorado Springs. They received kickbacks from the organization to allow Grove trucks to stop there. Later, Jose Rodriguez was the only one who ended up getting indicted because he was present at a lot of the meetings with the Meraz's.

Once when observing the trucks, we saw a tire being taken off and replaced with a new one. We knew what was going on. There had to be drugs in the tire they removed. Since we weren't the police, there wasn't much we could do but document what we saw and take the information to Larry. He was in charge of this case, and we took everything we found to him.

When Larry got the information about the tire exchanges at the tire shop on our side of the border, he set up an operation. He had an undercover RV he used for close and overnight surveillance. It was stored near the tire company, and Larry took it right to the tire place and monitored the comings and goings of all vehicles. He saw the Grande trucks going in and out of the port of entry and stopping at the shop regularly. They were exchanging at least one tire each time. After a while, Larry didn't see their trucks coming in anymore. *It was a daily routine, and it stopped! Why did that happen? Rodriguez's Tire Shop must know Larry is watching them.*

Once again, who knew Larry had the RV doing surveillance on the Rodriguez operation? He'd had to get permission from his office to set up the surveillance near the tire shop. So others in his office knew what he was doing, but no one else. Norman and Jorge were both very close to a U.S. customs agent. Larry wasn't sure but thought maybe someone in his office told a customs agent about the operations. He just wasn't sure who it could be.

<><><>

Yuma, AZ
Larry

The Grande warehouse in Yuma was a huge building with one large room and a high ceiling. I asked Frank Grover for permission to set up video cameras inside and outside.

Late one Sunday night, with the help of a local cop I trusted, we installed two cameras to watch trucks coming and going. One was placed inside and the other up high on the water tower overlooking the outside of the warehouse. I wanted to see if something was being switched at this location from one truck to another or to a car.

The next day, one of the truck drivers went straight up to the top of the warehouse and put his eyeball up to the video camera. I was wondering if there was a leak in law enforcement: *Where was this coming from? Could it be from my office? How did the truck driver know about the camera up there?*

<><><>

San Luis, AZ

The following week I found out that Pedro and Enano were staying alive because they were snorting cocaine with Olegario and Oscar. This was while the Meraz brothers were bragging about the agents they tried to kill, "Don't worry, we can get anyone or anything across the border and get whatever information we need because we have a niece who works at the border."[85]

DEA agent Richard (Richie) Fass was killed while working undercover in 1994 in Phoenix, Arizona. [86] Authorities were pretty sure it was Augusto Vasquez Mendoza who murdered him. Later that same day, Highway Patrol officers stopped and detained

98

Augusto's wife and her brother traveling to Yuma into Mexico. They were trying to escape into San Luis to avoid the DEA. Larry and another agent took custody of Augusto's wife and her brother from the State Troopers and put them in the back seat of the agent's car.[87]

While driving to San Luis, Augusto's wife and her brother refused to answer questions when I asked about the whereabouts of Augusto. She was almost nine months pregnant and continued to rub her huge belly and complain to me of sharp pains. She started crying out loud. I was so mad I wanted to slap the shit out of her. If only I had the Commandant with me.

Her brother was crying because of the intense questioning from me and the other agent. I told the agent to pull over to an isolated area next to a lemon grove a few miles away from the entrance to the Mexican border. The agent stopped, and I reached for a ketchup baggie from the glove compartment. I opened the door and whispered to the agent, "I'm taking this girl into the grove. I'll handcuff her to a lemon tree. Then I'll shoot one round from my .38-revolver into the air and smear the ketchup on my face and chest. When I return to the car without her, her brother will think I have blood on me. Then I'll jerk him out of the car, and he'll tell me where Augusto is."

As I got out of the car, dragging the screaming girl, her brother started crying for help. The agent yelled at him, "Don't Larry. The girl could have a miscarriage and lose the baby."

I thought about the way her husband had planned to kill Richie. I looked at the agent with anger, "She and her brother helped kill Richie."

I took her back to the car and pushed her into the backseat next to her brother. They were both screaming and crying. I wished I had the Mexican law enforcement with us because they could get the answers we wanted. She finally told us where the killer was hiding in Mexico.

We dropped Augusto's wife and her brother off at a trailer Augusto rented in San Luis, AZ. Then we immediately set up listening devices on the trailer. The next day, Augusto's wife and her brother disappeared into San Luis, Mexico. They were never seen again. Oscar told Pedro and Enano they knew Augusto's wife and her brother were in San Luis, Mexico but Augusto was not with them. Pedro asked, "Who is Augusto?"

Oscar said, "We don't want DEA to focus on us. Oscar mentioned that it was why Augusto's wife and brother-in-law are no longer in San Luis. They hope one of the shooters doesn't come to San Luis because they don't want DEA to focus on them, while they're looking for Richie Fass's killers."

Augusto Vasquez Mendoza became one of FBI's most wanted fugitive. He was captured and prosecuted in 2000.[88]

<><><>

Yuma, AZ

All this detail about the Meraz brothers was given over to Immigration and Naturalization Service (INS). The Meraz Organization had four different people working at the border who helped them. Two were dog handlers who didn't just go to jail; they went to prison. I told a Border Agent Internal Affairs, "You need to get the Meraz niece away from the port of entry and anyone else connected to the Meraz's. If you're not going to fire her, then get her away from the San Luis border. We've got a lot of information on her." Nothing was ever done by INS to remove her.

I found out from the investigators that Norman was my leak, indirectly. I couldn't believe my partner, Norman, was the corrupt agent. He had been talking to customs agents about the Meraz investigations. According to the private investigators, he was telling some agents outside the office what I was doing and what was happening in my investigation. Jeff and Randy didn't believe he was intentionally sabotaging the case. I wasn't sure, but I did have a bad leak in my office.

The Meraz's were well connected in Yuma area law enforcement. Some of the guys I knew in the community were related to the Meraz's and the corruption at the border. Jeff and Randy had their theories but couldn't verify if Norman was the leak. However, he could have unknowingly been sharing information that got back to the Meraz's. The agents in my office later backed out of helping me on the Meraz case because the heat from the US Attorney's office was coming down so hard on anyone connected to the case. No one in my office ever told me about any conversations with other law enforcement outside of DEA. But I knew if I worked with these guys, I would find the leak. If I continued to work with the private investigators on the case, my chance for career advancement was going to be unlikely.

A lot of people were involved here. It wasn't just about the Meraz's. It was also about the Chinese. And it was becoming very personal to me. Same with Jeff, Randy, Erik, and John. It's just the way it was in this business. I was working other cases at the same time and could have let this one go, but how could I after the relationships I'd built with the private investigators? They were giving me all kinds of information and intel to support my case, and we were becoming close friends.

<><><>

Colorado Springs, CO

Erik and I had been following the car of a relative of Enrique Medina. We wanted more information about their involvement with the Meraz organization and their connections in Colorado Springs.

Erik's father, Rolf, retired from the California Department of Motor Vehicles and worked for Jerry. Rolf accompanied me to meet with the Colorado Springs DEA. Jose Jonas Rodriguez was from there, and the DEA ran a case on Rodriguez.

Larry was watching Jose's wife. The PIs did not know why I needed to be in Colorado then. The PIs knew of a connection with Jose and his wife but weren't sure what connection would be revealed. We told Larry, "You need to go there and check it out.

101

There are many of the trucks going to Colorado Springs with furniture and drugs."

Rolf and I flew to Colorado Springs and went straight to the hotel. Larry got to travel with us and hang out when we weren't working. He flew in to meet us and stayed at the same hotel. Rolf and I shared a room, and Larry had his own room.

Larry, Rolf, and I were going to meet in the morning at the Colorado Springs DEA office to go over the Rodriguez and Jonas family connections to the Meraz's. Enrique Medina's brother was married to one of the Jonas sisters and Enrique was Oswaldo Meraz's brother-in-law.

Since our meeting wasn't until morning, the three of us decided to go down to the bar and have a couple of drinks. We were still wearing our suits, and I wore suspenders with mine.

After a few drinks, Rolf said to Larry and me, "You guys, I'm going to go but you ahead and stay. Don't get yourselves in trouble!"

A federal agent, and a private investigator. What kind of trouble could we cause?

Rolf stopped at the bar and said to the bartender, "If these two get out of hand, here's my room number."

Half the people in the bar were Air Force cadets. There were also some young girls walking around looking for their future husbands. They weren't looking for me. It was karaoke night, and I decided to go up and sing. While I was singing, the cadets in the back started making fun of me. I was shitfaced or at least, getting there and said, "What are you bald motherfuckers laughing at? Shut the fuck up!" I kept on singing, but the cadets wouldn't shut up.

Larry was thinking: Oh boy, here he goes! Jeff is trying to pick up a girl and wondering why he can't.

After I finally stopped singing, I returned to the table. Later, I was just sitting there, really depressed, telling Larry that I wanted to impress the girl who was waiting on us.

Larry said, "Here, you take my badge over to her. Show it to her, tell her you're a cop, and you want to get to know her!"

Larry told Jerry and Rolf later, "Sure enough, Jeff went over there. Flashed that damn badge and came back, smiling like a canary. He didn't get the girl, but he was really pleased with how the badge worked."

I wanted to keep the badge, "Can I have it?"

The waitress came over, and we flirted for a few minutes. She finally let me know she had a boyfriend.

Larry said, "What?"

"Yeah, he's very good to me," she stated.

"Then, why would you flirt with someone like Jeff if you have a boyfriend?"

"Who are you to say who I should flirt with?"

Larry flashed his badge and said, "I'm an authority on the subject. He's my partner, he's supposed to shut me up, but he wanted to keep my badge so he could impress you."

She just walked away.

While we were sitting there, things started escalating between the cadets and me. They were yelling at me, "What are you doing? You can't sing."

The bartender called Rolf's room to let him know things were getting out of hand. He told Larry and me that Rolf was on his way down to meet us in the lobby.

I continued with my song.

The Cadets continued to hassle me, "Who do you think you are? Frank Sinatra? You've got to do better than that."

I stood up and pulled on my suspenders and smiled at them, then I returned to Larry and said, "I heard that the Colorado Springs law enforcement was called. Someone called Rolf and told him that you and I are in the lobby."

Larry and I walked out to the lobby where some of the cadets were waiting.

Two Colorado Springs law enforcement officers came over to us. "Hi, guys. Is everything okay?"

Larry said, "Yeah, I'm a federal agent, and I'm going to bed."

"Okay!"

Then Rolf said, "Jeff, you're with me!"

When Jerry heard about what happened, he was hot and fired up! "You two!"

Of course, I was in trouble again! Not Larry because he was a DEA agent.

Chapter 15: Meeting the Commandanté; *Yuma, AZ*

1994, Larry

We needed to get the Meraz's indicted quickly because more people in the law enforcement community were getting involved in my investigation. More people at the POE were catching wind of the case.

Things were happening very fast and all at once. The private investigators were in Yuma every week, working on the case. Sometimes it was Jeff and Erik, or Randy or John would join Jeff. It was a multi-faceted project. Randy and John were usually working on another part of the case in Fresno or Los Angeles. They provided me with lots of intelligence to use to build the case against the Meraz brothers using Grove Manufacturing to smuggle drugs into the U.S.

I got to know Jeff and Randy, as well as the other PIs. I'm a professional, I already knew what was going on, and they worked together as a team. Jeff jumped into narcotics and into a whole new world where it's very easy to cross the line to the dark side. I was worried he was going to fall into that dark way of life, especially with the women he used as sources.

Many of Jeff's informants were the wives or informants of law enforcement officers. Jeff didn't necessarily go looking for trouble, but he was eager to get the information from them. If it meant he had to flirt with them to get the information, then that's what he did. His uncle was instrumental in getting him started and keeping him using the women for all the information he could get.

I'm thankful I had my wife close to me. I was close to home. These other guys were away from home and more easily drawn into the dark side to access information. I worried about what it could do to them.

I started receiving feedback from sources and CIs that identified experienced narcotics agents like corrupt customs agent Peter Aduana and a San Luis, Arizona, police officer, Tom Diaz.

The corrupt customs agent was the nicest guy in the world, but Jeff's intelligence on him was dirty as hell, big time corruption. However, I got along with the customs agent. Former Sheriff Jack Pollard told me to stay away from the crooked police officer because he was already under investigation for corruption.

Jeff and Randy sat down with hand-held scanners bought from Radio Shack and figured out all the frequencies for phone lines at Grande and other companies in the area. They made up a sheet of information about specific individuals. When a call came through, they could look on the sheet and determine whose line it was and record what they were saying on their mini-cassette recorders.

Sometimes Jeff and Erik sat at the border with the scanners. These scanners could pick up certain radio frequencies. In the '90s, they didn't have all the encryption capabilities that cell phones have today. During the case, a lot of our technology changed. The scanners no longer worked when phone calls became encrypted.

When they were watching trucks coming across the border in San Luis, they got hits that sounded like phone conversations. A few were in English. They were able to hear both sides of the conversation. They started marking and recording them. Soon they were recognizing some of the things going on and could identify which were coming in or going out of Grande Manufacturing.

Whenever Enrique made a call, even in Spanish, they would record it. They didn't know what the Spanish calls were about, but they later had them transcribed and translated. Anytime he mentioned shrimp; they were able to hear it on the airwave transmissions. It was not really a wiretap, and it did allow them to record the calls.

Which I didn't want to know! They had the green light from the owner for Grande and their attorneys.

One recording captured was between Ed Pastor, the Arizona State Senator, and the Meraz cartel.

Jeff and Erik were pretty patriotic guys, so they were outraged, thinking: *This isn't right!*

They told me, "Listen to what we've got here!" They shared their recording.

I called FBI Mark Spencer. Mark came to my office and picked up the tape.

Two weeks later, when we hadn't heard anything, I called Mark and asked, "What's going on with the tape I gave you?" Mark told me he ran this up the pole, and nobody in the United States government wanted to touch it. So that just fizzled out.

<><><>

After delving into the Meraz case, the U.S. Attorney's office sent me a letter from Richard Dreamer. Richard was very appreciative of the work I was doing on the case. "Your dedication to the case is outstanding, and hopefully, your efforts will begin to bring dividends."[89] Richard continued to encourage me to push United States Customs toward prosecution and close the case. Richard wanted to bring the Meraz case to an end quickly.

I felt uneasy because AUSA Dreamer and I were not always on the same page. He didn't support me working with the private investigators and their information.

<><><>

San Luis, Mexico
Larry

Norman asked me to go with him to meet with the Federal Commandanté in San Luis, Mexico. The Commandanté called about a small Cessna aircraft that crashed in the desert in El Golfo, near the fishing village where Oswaldo had his shrimp business. The small plane was loaded with cocaine. I knew the Federal Commandanté was a corrupt law enforcement officer who worked closely with the Meraz brothers. Norman said he'd met him before and had given him several boxes of 45-caliber ammunition. On one occasion he gave him an apple pie in exchange for information on drug traffickers in Mexico. I was wondering: *Why would my partner trust a corrupt Commandanté?*

Norman and I arrived at the Mexico Federal Police station and met the Commandanté in San Luis, Sonora, Mexico. The Commandanté he would take us to the crashed plane. It was about a 2½ hour drive south of San Luis in El Golfo. While we were at the police station, I observed a young man being slapped in the face several times by the Federales. The man's wife was watching the Federales hitting her husband. Then they moved her to another location inside the building. I had heard from informants and witnesses that corrupted Mexican cops would take advantage of a woman for sexual pleasure. Unfortunately, I knew what she was in for. The Commandanté said, "Let's go!" Norman and I jumped into the back seat of a black SUV with the Commandanté and his driver. The driver was traveling very fast through the town of San Luis, Mexico, followed by several black SUVs with armed plainclothes federal police. We finally arrived at an isolated desert area where the plane had crashed. I noticed it was burned down to the metal. The plane had carried coke, but someone had unloaded it before we arrived. He was smiling as he spoke of the disappearing coke. I was thinking to myself: *What's really going on? Without a doubt, the Commandanté knows where the cocaine is and who has it.*

The Commandanté had a small black camera in his hand and wanted to take a picture of me, no one else, without my shirt, as he told Norman in Spanish. Here I was, in the middle of nowhere at a burned-out desert crash site in Mexico with a corrupt Commandanté, near Oswaldo's shrimp business. I can't even speak Spanish fluently, especially the Mexican slang.

I looked directly at the Commandanté's bulging eyes and said to Norman, "I want the Commandanté to understand that if he wants a picture of me with my shirt off, then his law enforcement officers, all 12 of them, and you too, are going to take their shirts and we all take a picture together. You know, like a big happy family out in the middle of the 120° F desert."

Norman nervously translated what I said to the Commandanté. The other Mexican officers laughed, and the Commandanté smiled. He started to laugh and put the camera to his face. Then he told everyone to take off their shirts, including me. I took my shirt off thinking: *I'm the only white skinned dude out here in this desert!* The Commandanté took several pictures of Norman and me, focusing on me.

It was clear in the hot desert sun; the Mexican Commandanté knew what happened to the plane and who had the drugs. He invited me over to Oswaldo's cantina in El Golfo for lunch – the only restaurant in the village. How could I say "no" to the Commandanté in the middle of the desert, surrounded by armed Federales?

At Owasldo's Cantina, "We are all eating tiger shrimp!" announced the Commandantée.

I was wondering: Who'll pay the bill? It's not going to be the Commandanté or me.

At the restaurant, we all drank a few Coronas and ate some of the biggest shrimp I'd ever seen. Commandanté shouted again, "The shrimp is tiger shrimp. The best!" No one paid the bill; it was free.

Norman and I arrived back at the border at San Luis late that night. I thought to myself; *It's a wonderful feeling to cross into the United States from Mexico. Thank God, I'm alive!* Now the Meraz brothers have a picture of me. The Meraz's and their traffickers can recognize me when they see me follow them in Yuma and near the border. It was extremely dangerous for me. I could be kidnapped and killed.

But I wasn't afraid of the criminals. I was more cautious of the government and working with other agents and law enforcement. I wasn't thinking of officials in Mexico, but my own people in law enforcement.

Many times, I would see the investigators following me around on both sides of the border. I asked them to keep me in their sights. They would follow me, and I would follow them. It was all about staying alive.

Chapter 16: A Constant Adventure

1992-1996

This case was a constant adventure for the Pearce Investigators. They were young guys experiencing many crazy things. Sometimes it was even amusing!

<><><>

Yuma, AZ
Randy

We were always getting into trouble with Jerry. John, Erik, and I would go shopping and buy bathing suits, cigars, etc. and charge it to our American Express card with the Pearce Corporation name on it. When we turned in our expense reports, the secretary said, "You guys can't be buying this stuff on the American Express card!" John responded, "I'll do what I want to do because my last name is on the door."

We were at Yuma County courthouse, going over various drug cases. We would flirt with the girls there to get better access to the information we needed. The girls would ask, "Are you DEA?"

"We can't tell you." It wasn't a denial. We just didn't say it.

One of the girls was talking with another DEA guy and said, "You know those two new DEA guys are pretty cool. You work with them, right?"

He said, "No, but thanks for the information."

That happened before we got really close to Larry. Larry called Jerry the next morning. When Jeff and I walked into the office, Jerry was on the phone. Jerry motioned to us to come in.

To Jerry's credit, he backed us. He told Larry, "There's no way in hell my boys would say they're DEA."

Larry's response was, "Okay, I'm just letting you know what I heard. Make sure they don't misinform people."

Jerry got off the phone, turned to us and said, "What the hell are you guys doing?"

"Jerry, we never said it. They just assumed!"

It's a small town with only three DEA agents. There was no mistaking who the girl was talking about.

Norman was upset that we were claiming we were DEA agents. So after that, we decided, "Oh well, we get in trouble for it anyway!" and kept allowing people to assume what they wanted.

Sometimes, we showed our company American Express card with the name Pearce Corporation, and people thought it said, "Peace Corps." They would ask, "If you're in the Peace Corps, what are you doing here? Shouldn't you be in the Amazon jungle or something?"

We would respond, "No, we're Peace Corps investigators." That usually worked.

I was the only non-family member of the core group working for Pearce, but he didn't treat me any better or worse than the others. He was an asshole to everyone, but he was always fair!

Jeff's response to that was, "Oh yeah, he treats everybody equally! When it's my time to go, it's my time to go. That was after the case was pretty much done, anyway."

<><><>

Conway, AR
Jeff

In 1993, Randy and I went to do some surveillance at the Grove Manufacturing plant. We went there to see if we could find additional information about the 18-wheeler trucks owned by the maquiladora that were coming to Conway, Arkansas. Many trucks suspected and moving large quantities of narcotics were hiding in Arkansas. The plant is about two and a half hours from Mena, Arkansas.

We flew into Shreveport, Louisiana, because we had a meeting with some guys connected to Grove Manufacturing. I also had to meet a newspaper reporter and collect information on another case.

After that, we quickly drove to Conway. When we arrived, we looked for a hotel and found one on the Arkansas River. It was a nice place, and Bill Clinton often stayed there. But our per diem didn't allow us to spend more than $100 per night.

We knew we couldn't afford it. But we knew a way to get around that problem. We'd already been in trouble for implying we were DEA although we never actually came right out and said it. And we didn't want to start now.

When we got inside, I asked the clerk, "How much are the rooms for a night?"

"Rooms start at $300 a night," she said.

I showed her my credentials. "I'm a United States Marshal, now, how much?"

"Sixty bucks a night."

"We'll take it."

Larry jokingly said to us later, "Why didn't you just say you were DEA? It would have been a lot easier." Then he added, "A lot of people in law enforcement already think your agents anyway."

I told him, "Because we didn't want to get in trouble again."

We had a great room overlooking the Arkansas River. When we were going to get something to eat, we noticed there was a high school reunion in the ballroom.

Randy said, "I'm going to the reunion."

"What do you mean? You don't know any of these people!"

He said, "I'm going to hang out with some girls!"

He walked over to the table with name badges. There were maybe four badges left. One of them had a guy's name on it. The rest were girl's names.

Randy said, "The dude probably didn't show." He took it and slapped it on. Then he walked into the ballroom.

I thought, *Well, I want to go, too.* So, I showed my ID and said, "Hotel security."

It was a three-day reunion with activities in the evenings. We could have some fun and not miss any of our daytime duties. We picked up a couple of girls and took them to dinner at the big steamboat restaurant across the way.

He got into the class picture up on stage. On the third day, one of the guys from the reunion confronted Randy and said, "They know you're not Norm."

Randy responded, "How do they know that?"

"Norm is not white!"

There were several times we did things just to have fun on our days off. They gave us a sense of relief from the stress of our work.

We later got into it with Jerry on the phone: "You guys aren't doing anything but goofing off over there!"

"No, we've been working hard!" And we were! We observed trucks during the day and then joined the reunion activities in the evenings.

I told Randy, "He wants us to come home tomorrow!"

We made flight arrangements to leave in the morning about 9:00 a.m. out of Shreveport. It was around 6:00 a.m. when we woke up, and we had a 200-mile drive. We rented a Thunderbird.

I said, "I'm driving." I drove about 120 mph on a two-lane highway from Arkansas to Louisiana. We were flying along, and Randy was half asleep in the passenger seat. There was a center divider with just grass and sitting in the middle of it was a highway patrol car. As I went speeding by, I could see the officer pointing at me!

I hit Randy and said, "Randy! Randy, wake up."

"What?"

"Randy, I'm going to jail!"

I kept up my speed. It took a good ten miles for that cop to catch up to us. I slowed down, pulled over, and waited for the cop to pull up. We saw him speeding past and whip around ahead of us. Then he came up behind us at about five car lengths and said on the loudspeaker, "Get out of the car and come to me!"

114

In Arkansas, the officers don't come to the car – you need to walk back to them.

Randy and I were discussing how we were going to get the car back to the rental place, get checked in, and try not to miss the flight. I stepped out of the car and approached the officer. I was thinking to myself: *I'm sure he's 6'3". A big white, corn-fed, son-of-a-gun!*

Jeff walked up to him, dressed in his suit.

Randy was thinking: We're going to get arrested! We're going to jail!

"What in the fuck possessed you to be flying by at that speed?"

"We need to get to the airport…"

He interrupted me, "I don't give a fuck what you have to do! What are you doing in this town, dressed in a suit and all this?"

"Sir, I'm a private investigator."

As soon as I said that he said, "Really? What's that like?"

"Yeah, we're working on a narcotics case over here and trying to get some information."

He looked at his watch and said, "I'll tell you what, you follow me, I'll keep it below 85 mph, and we'll get you to the airport in time for your flight."

As we drove behind him, the officer put his lights on a couple of times and led us to the airport. We couldn't believe it. We made it on time to turn in our rental car and catch our flight.

<><><>
Yuma, AZ
Jeff

Jack Pollard retired after 35 years as Sheriff of Yuma County. His undersheriff was Henry Utah. When Jack retired, Henry took over as interim chief until the next sheriff was appointed. Henry was later appointed sheriff. Jack Pollard introduced Erik and me to Henry,

Jack had been sheriff so long that he knew about the Meraz's and the work we were doing. He was a wealth of information for us, and we relied on him for a lot of information.

Jack was then contacted to serve as interim chief for the San Luis Police Department (SLPD), the border police station. Pollard initially introduced Erik and me to Police Officer Tom Diaz at Round Table Pizza in San Luis. Officer Diaz worked with Pollard at SLPD. When we first met, Jack had told us, "Whatever you guys need, let me know, and I'll make sure you get it."

I told Jack, "You've been so helpful to us. What are we going to do when you leave?

Jack responded, "I can fix that!"

"How's that?"

"Raise your right hand" he swore Erik and I in as officers of the SLPD. We got IDs, a badge, the whole nine yards. So now we were civilian investigators, sworn in as police officers. Essentially, we were law enforcement!

Jeffrey A Pearce
San Luis Police, Arizona

We didn't go to Arizona Law Enforcement Academy (ALEA) where the others had gone for training. As chief of police, Jack had the authorization to swear in anyone and gave us our own credentials.

Jack was there for only a few months until Bill Summers became the new chief of police. Jack introduced us, and when he left, we continued to work with Bill Summers and Tom Diaz.

After leaving SLPD, Jack Pollard went to work at the Attorney General's office in Yuma. Erik and I would meet with Jack at his office in the mornings for coffee and brief him. He gave us a key to his office since he wasn't in the office every day. He

116

told us, "There's another room here you guys can use to come in and work. You can use the copy machine and whatever else you need."

He provided us with a hand-held radio with sheriff's department dispatch. We also got radios we rented every month from a communications company across the street from the Yuma airport. When we knew we were going to need the radios for the week, we would stop by, pick them up on our way into town, and put them in our vehicle. We could communicate back and forth. These radios were on repeaters that covered an area from Yuma County to Phoenix. At the end of the week, we dropped them off to store until the next time we needed them.

The Cocopah Indian Reservation had their own law enforcement, the Cocopah Tribal Police Department. Grove trucks were using Indian land to move contraband through. The only investigators allowed on the reservation for any information was the tribal police or FBI. We couldn't get anything from FBI Agent Mark Spencer because he didn't cooperate

Jeffrey A Pearce
Cocopah Tribal Police

with us. Jack Pollard introduced us to Black Hawk Nuka, the tribal police under-chief and one of the law enforcement officers in charge. When Erik and I mentioned to Black Hawk they had some information we wanted to pursue on the reservation, he said, "I can help you with that. Please raise your right hand." He made us tribal police officers and gave us IDs signed by the chief of police.

With credentials from SLPD and the Cocopah Tribal PD, stated our terms were indefinite. We are still police officers with both departments, even now. We don't use our IDs these days, but technically we're still officers.

According to Larry, Norman was jealous of our law enforcement badges. He had worked on the Indian reservation as a traveling sheriff and couldn't understand why we were given badges.

He asked Larry, "How did they get those?"

Larry told him, "I don't know. Sheriff Pollard likes the boys a lot!" And he really did. According to a report Larry made to Yuma in late 1990, FBI Mark Spencer identified former Sheriff Pollard as being under investigation for corruption. Larry later realized that it was bullshit and Pollard was getting close to the truth about political corruption connected with individual officers.

Officer Tom Diaz was a very friendly guy. We took to him, and he took to us. We got him involved with the Meraz case and with the federal government. We shared some information with Johnny Perez about the Meraz and Grande, too.

Pollard told Larry, "I'd stay away from Johnny Perez. He's under investigation for corruption and for being a possible snitch for the FBI." Pollard would vouch for Jeff and Erik, but he didn't trust Johnny. Pollard became a good friend to Larry, Jeff, Randy, Erik, and John.

<><><>

A month later, Jerry was planning to fly down to Yuma. He wanted to meet with Randy, John, and I to see how things were going.

He called ahead and told me, "Set me up! Get me a room where you're staying."

We were at the Parkside Inn. Randy and John went to the office to make a reservation for him, and they came back out laughing their heads off.

I asked, "What happened?"

"We put that fucker in a handicapped room."

"You did what? Dudes! He's going to lose his mind!"

When Jerry got to the airport, he called us to pick him up.

He didn't want to go to his room right away. As usual, he wanted to find a place to have coffee and pie, or a meal.

I shared a room with Erik and Randy shared with John. When we finally went to bed, we hadn't heard anything from Jerry. We expected our phones to ring, or something.

The next morning, we all met at the coffee shop downstairs for breakfast. Jerry came up to us, saying, "You fuckers! Really funny! The light switches were down here (pointing waist high), but the chair in the shower, I really enjoyed that!"

I asked, "Do you want us to get you a different room?"

"No, I want to stay there! Just leave it."

Dianne DeMille PhD, Larry Hardin, Jeffrey Pearce, Randy Torgerson

Chapter 17: Meetings in Yuma, AZ

1992-1996, Jeff

The Skyview Bar was painted pink, so we called it the "Pink Panther." It was located right next to the DEA office. While Erik and I were in Yuma, we would drop in for a few belts after our workday. Often, when we arrived in town around noon, after picking up our car, we would stop by to see if Jack Pollard's truck was parked at the Pink Panther. If he was there, we would stop in and have lunch and a beer with him.

We got to know the owner and regulars of the Skyview. Management knew Jack Pollard personally and always had a table waiting for him when he walked in. Then they'd immediately present him with his drink, a Beefeater. Pollard was a great guy, wore a big cowboy hat, very straight. If he didn't like you, he didn't like you. But if he liked you, you had a good friend for life. Norman was one of the guys he didn't really like.

I was 5' 9" and wore my cowboy boots and hat. My blue jeans were so tight that I couldn't bend over without falling. I had to fit in!

Larry was usually sitting at the bar after work and told everyone that when I came in, "He'd walk up behind me and I'd see him in the mirror. Jeff smiled at me like a dead possum!" We had a great time there.

One of the regulars at the Pink Panther was a meat distributor. If the meat didn't sell after a certain number of days, it would be taken off the shelf and destroyed. The meat was excellent! There was nothing wrong with it.

One day, I asked him, "So, what are you going to do with all that meat?"

"I'm going to throw it away."

"You don't give it to the homeless or something?"

"No, we just throw it away."

"I'll tell you what, I'll buy you a couple of beers, and you can kick some meat our way."

"Okay."

I bought the meat man a couple of beers, and we went out to the back of his truck. He had several boxes filled with steaks, ribs, and sausage and gave us a full box. We made this a weekly deal.

Jack Pollard had a very nice five-acre ranch with horses. I would hook up with him and go out to the ranch and put the meat in Jack Pollard's freezer. After a while, there'd be so much frozen meat we had to do something with it. So we put on a community barbeque. Everyone loved it!

<><><>

Over the weeks, months, and years, we developed our own network of informants. When I flew in on Monday mornings, Avis would have my vehicle ready. That was how well-connected we were.

We had informants in Mexico, Arizona, and California. One of Jeff's informants in Yuma came from Mexico. He was a United States citizen, served in Vietnam, and was a real hero. He became a fantastic informant! He worked as a drug guard for the Meraz's, but he was still very true to the U.S. That relationship got a little dicey. Erik and I probably met with him too often, and word got around. Larry said, "The vet was indeed a real hero according to military records. He was a Marine, wounded twice in Vietnam, saving the lives of his buddies. He was promoted from a field commission to Lieutenant.

Erik and I had some other informants within Grande. One was Javier Pina, chief security officer, and a woman in human resources. She was a beautiful girl, white with red hair, and she spoke perfect Spanish. We went to her house to investigate furniture theft. As our relationship grew and we developed trust, she became more involved. One night she called me and said "Aldo Campo, the plant manager at Grove Manufacturing, left his briefcase at the office and wants me to bring it across the border and drop it off at his house. What do you want me to do?"

I told her, "Bring it here; we're going to make copies of everything in it first."

She met me in town, and we copied every document in the briefcase. We shut it up and then she delivered it to Aldo's house at the U.S.-Yuma border. He had stuff in there on his own trucking company. He was essentially running another business in Mexico hauling furniture and selling it without the owner's consent. There were all kinds of information in the briefcase we could use.

I had other sources at the electric company in town. I could walk into the office, hand them a list of addresses and say, "I want all the information on these addresses." They would print out their full information for everyone on the list, including social security numbers, references, and everything else. It was like a little biography of people living at each address.

I went out of my way to get information any way I could. If that meant flirting with the county clerk to get it, then that's what I did. The others did the same thing, but not as much as me.

I worked mainly with Larry, but no one else from DEA. That was the way Larry wanted it. I had informants, not quite the level of Larry's, who knew key players of the Meraz organization. I gave information to Larry about Mario Camaron, a CIA agent, but Larry wouldn't provide anything to me. If I was in danger of getting too close to the Meraz brothers, then Larry would tell me. It was a cat-and-mouse game between Larry and me all the time.

Erik and I told Larry about weapons brought across the border. Camaron was involved. Larry verified the information with a customs agent who told him, "Camaron will give you a lot of problems on your Meraz case!" The agent advised Larry to stay away from Camaron because of his connections with the CIA.

A week before, an Arizona Highway Patrol agent had given Larry the name of Mario Camaron, who had a shrimp business in Mexico. Larry heard the name popping up all over the place from law enforcement sources and informants in the Yuma County area. Camaron was connected with the CIA for weapons used by the Meraz brothers. Larry didn't want to deal with the "Spooks" (CIA). He just wanted to stay focused, with blinders, on the Meraz organization, the murders, and attempted killings. But Larry couldn't do that because he kept hitting one roadblock after another from United States Attorney Richard Dreamer as he tried to continue the investigation.

Larry told Pedro to arrange a meeting with Camaron to get information about the Meraz drug business.

Pedro and Enano later met with Camaron to discuss their shrimp business in Mexico. Camaron told Pedro to be careful with Olegario. He discussed nothing else with Pedro. That was the CIs' last meeting with Camaron. Larry told the CIs to stay away from him.

Erik, John, and I followed people like Mario Camaron, who often stayed at the Shilo Inn in Yuma. Larry didn't want to target Camaron because of his connections with the CIA.

<><><>

Yuma, AZ

Larry

Back then, cell phones weren't like what they are now. At most of the hotels, you could make calls from the room and then receive a bill at the end of the stay with a list of the phone numbers called.

I wouldn't be able to get this sort of information without some form of search warrant or subpoena. Jeff would befriend the desk clerk. It would take a couple of weeks to get them where they felt comfortable enough to help him out.

The clerks would print out whatever Jeff wanted. He would tell them, "I need a list of who he called, how he paid, etc. And every time he comes in, I want to know, this, this, this..."

Jeff would come into the hotel, and the clerks would have a folder ready for him. Soon we started getting information about the phone calls made by many of the people we were surveilling.

Imagine this at every hotel in Yuma! Not all of them, but a majority of them where he developed a relationship to get the information he wanted.

It was the same thing with the girls at the County Courthouse Clerk's Office. His uncle was the worst. He encouraged Jeff! Jerry told him, "Just do what you do best, and we'll get the information."

Jeff used to have the girls meet him at the hotels during happy hours, have drinks, develop relationships, then he would get whatever he wanted.

Law enforcement would tell me Jeff was over at the such and such hotel. He didn't have a good reputation with most of the guys in the law enforcement community in town, maybe with the women, but not with the men, especially law enforcement. They knew when Jeff was in town!

Dianne DeMille PhD, Larry Hardin, Jeffrey Pearce, Randy Torgerson

Chapter 18: Concerns About Jeff; Yuma, AZ

1994, Jeff

Erik Hansen worked with me during most of my time in Yuma. One day we walked out of the hotel room in the morning and drove down the street to our local coffee shop for breakfast. We drove into San Luis, Arizona, and saw that a San Luis PD officer, one of the corrupt officers, was following our informant. Somehow, he knew who our informant was.

There was a lineup of cars on our tail. An agent with the DEA was following the police officer, we were behind the DEA car, the FBI was following us, and there was one more car following the FBI car. We think the last one was someone with the CIA.

This one little town! We had a caravan! We kept going for about 15 minutes. Finally, we stopped and just started laughing. We said to each other, "This is ridiculous!" Then everyone scattered and got out of our way.

After that, whenever we went into San Luis, we would get up in the morning, have breakfast, and head to the border.

We made a call to Larry and told him, "If you don't put it in your computer, we think we'll be okay." The minute he entered our activities into the system, someone knew too much about what we were doing.

The other agencies believed that Larry had to be feeding us intelligence information because of what we knew about the Meraz operations. Criminals were working in the DEA too. Larry heard comments in his office that they couldn't believe we came up with the information we had on the Meraz organization.

<><><>

The following week, Erik and I flew to Los Angeles, following some of the guys from Grove Manufacturing. We left and flew back to Fresno on a Friday night. Erik had an old piece of luggage with his revolver in it. It was no big deal. This was before we had Transportation Security Administration (TSA) and full security at the airport. We could pack a revolver in the luggage without any problems.

The procedure was to declare that it was there, with a date on the form that was only good for that trip. Many times, the clerk was lazy and left the date blank. Since it was rarely checked, Erik and I left the date blank. That way, we didn't need to declare the gun every time we flew on that airline. If someone saw it, we would tell them we didn't realize it didn't have the date written on it.

This time, when the luggage shot out to the carousel, Erik's suitcase broke open as it landed on the belt. All his belongings scattered, and the revolver went flying across the floor! That scared everyone around us. The police were called. Erik explained how the luggage had burst open. He showed the paperwork for carrying the revolver, and the officers just wrote up a report, and that was it.

And, of course, Erik and I got in trouble with Jerry.

There was another time when Erik and I were flying back to Fresno, and Erik had an old warrant for his arrest. When we arrived in Fresno, officers found a handgun in his checked luggage. The police were called. When they ran Erik's name through the system, they booked him into the old jail in Fresno. The old warrant was for some traffic situation. It was nothing major, and they released him right away.

◇◇◇

There was often a lot of conflict between Jerry and me, as well as the other investigators. I felt like I had to continue to push.

I lived in Yuma for five years on and off. I was under a lot of pressure from Uncle Jerry when he would tell me, "If this case folds, then we're going to have to fold, too. I'm going to have to drop my rate. And I'm going to have to cut people's pay."

Uncle Jerry would make other comments like, "Okay, you guys are now on hourly rates." It was great for me because I was working some 16-17-hour days and getting some large paychecks.

Then he told me, "Okay, we're going to put you back on salary." That's when I stopped working for more than eight-hour days.

After a week of working under these new conditions, Uncle Jerry asked, "Why am I not getting the same production out of you?"

"It's very simple. You're not paying me for it."

Randy said, "In reality, we may have stopped after eight hours on a couple of days, but we were into the case, especially Jeff. We would think we were done for the day and about to go for dinner and try to relax. Then we'd get a page. That meant we had to meet somebody or do something. We didn't always count those hours."

Some issues I caused for myself. I often commented to the others that I wished I had never been involved in the case. I believed I was larger than life, and I thought I could do anything! I was probably fired six times in this case. That was normal.

I would challenge Uncle Jerry.

Randy responded, "Yeah, but that's Jerry! I didn't do anything wrong, and I was fired three times."

Jerry would yell at all of us, and we would have knocked-out, drag-out fights. Jerry would fire us and a day, or even just hours later would rehire us. Randy, John, Erik, and I had many conversations about keeping our jobs.

When talking about the case, I don't think anyone realized how hard our work really was. We had to keep the information fresh and up to date. We didn't care how many hours a day it took to do it. Jerry was making a mint. He had four or five of us working on the case at any one time. The client was charged $13,000 a week, and Jerry was only paying us a small wage. The client was paying all expenses and overhead, as well as our wages. That was my uncle! He didn't care about our marriages, our relationships, or our families. Uncle Jerry was a self-serving prick and did nothing but push, push, push! And he knew how to do it. When he couldn't sleep in the middle of the night, he would page us "911" to call him back from our hotel room.

In my 20s, getting $45,000 a year was a good living. For five years, Monday through Friday, every week I was gone from my family and sometimes I had to stay away for the weekend. Randy and John were gone from their families, too and Erik didn't have anybody, but his dirty socks. That was an inside joke about Erik.

We were pushed to our limits. Jerry had such a way of playing everyone against each other, manipulating situations. He didn't want alliances. He didn't want his investigators getting along with each other. He would start shit to get us fighting by saying, "You're in charge now." "I'm going to send you down there to work with Jeff's informants." "I'm going to send you over here." All he did was create chaos!

Jerry would go into Grove Manufacturing board meetings and drag me along to provide the information I had gathered, which was a tremendous amount because I knew this case inside and out. Then he would just sit there. He wanted a pat on the back. He would talk about how well he was doing and why they should continue to pay him this enormous amount of money.

Randy commented, "He did treat everyone equal; I'll give him that."

Yeah, because it was all about him. I don't want to sound vicious toward him, but he was no cakewalk. Jerry was a very charismatic and dynamic personality. He didn't take shit from anybody.

Anytime Larry appeared to be losing steam on the Meraz investigation, whatever the situation was, Jerry would get Larry on the phone and give him a pep talk. Or he'd send Larry a letter, to keep him going. Larry was part of his moneymaking machine. If the case kept going, he was going to continue to get paid. That was just the way Jerry worked.

<><><>

Larry

It was a cat-and-mouse game all the time. We didn't know what we didn't know! We thought we might win the battle because we thought we were doing well and building a lot of intelligence. We could end up destroying our own lives down the road.

Randy, Erik, John, and Jeff continued to cause issues for the Meraz organization. When Jack Pollard was SLPD Chief of Police, his lieutenant was the brother-in-law to Olegario Meraz, Elizabeth Nunez's husband. Jeff was always curious about him working at a police station on the border.

Larry often said, "Law enforcement in Yuma and San Luis always knew where I was, in my office or out on the streets. They could find me at the Best Western eating French fries and drinking tea. I protected Jeff, Randy, Erik, and John because I was DEA. They did more hard work and took more risks in this case than I did because I was working on other cases at the same time, too. There were times I'd be doing surveillance by myself, and they followed me around briefly. They were protecting me because they always felt like something was going to happen to me. There was a lot of law enforcement corruption, and I was feeling vulnerable."

Randy said, "I got the feeling local law enforcement thought we couldn't be private investigators because of the amount of information we were able to get about their operation. They thought we must be somebody else."

<> <> <>

Jeff

Gabriel Garza had been the police chief of SLPD until he was fired, and Jack Pollard became the interim chief. He lived in a motor home with his wife in San Luis. I went with Erik to talk to him. He seemed to be a decent enough guy. We didn't tell him much about what we were working on, but he indicated he wanted to provide us with information and knew some of the people involved with the Meraz's. He thought he could help us. We would meet Garza at different restaurants in Yuma regularly. He would bring his five-year-old daughter with him.

Garza had some issues with United States Customs at the time, specifically with Peter Aduana and a couple of other agents who were there. Garza couldn't stand Johnny Perez and thought he lost his job at SLPD because of him. Garza seemed to be a perfect candidate to learn about some of the corruption we were hearing about and had some good contacts. Erik and I started communicating with him and gave him a CI number.

I tried to keep tabs on what was going on. I met the chief of United States Customs, and when he found out that I was dealing with the Chief of Police in Yuma, he made a call to Henry Utah. They set up a meeting at the restaurant in the Chilton Hotel for my CI and me. Henry and the customs chief gave Gabriel Garza a wire to wear to the meeting. Then they parked down the street to listen in.

Aldo Campo, the plant manager of Grande Manufacturing, was running his own trucking company, Hoover Trucking. We were trying to gather information on Johnny Perez and the Hoover truck deliveries because Campo was diverting furniture from Grove Manufacturing, selling it on his own in Mexico, and using his Hoover trucks to transport. Our information confirmed that Johnny and Enrique Medina were part of it. Johnny had several telephone conversations with Aldo and Erik, and I had documented several discussions between the two of us.

We told Garza that Henry had been contacting the Meraz's through one of their nephews. We asked Garza, "How would you like to piss in Johnny Perez's cornflakes?"

Garza answered, "Of course."

I told him, "This is allegedly what he's doing. He's helping Aldo Campo transport furniture into the United States. Can you start looking into it and see what you can find out?"

One day, he came in to meet us at the Chilton Restaurant. He had his daughter with him as always. But he was nervous and sweaty.

"What's wrong with you?" I asked him. "Are you okay?"

"Yeah, yeah, I'm fine."

The guy was really nervous. Then, when I started talking about customs, Garza stood up, didn't say a word to us, and walked out of the meeting.

I mentioned to Erik, "He seemed a little off."

"Yeah, he did."

We didn't know what was going on.

Later, we heard from Larry that Customs had put a wire on Garza and sent him in to talk to us. When I confronted Garza, he confessed and said, "Yeah, but the wire didn't work because I was sweating too much. It didn't pick up anything."

That's when I knew they were investigating us. Other agents were trying to determine our tactics, techniques, what we had, and how we were getting it. Customs wanted to know what we knew. They couldn't figure out how we were coming up with the information we had.

No wonder Garza was nervous!

The customs agents were upset when they discovered they couldn't hear anything we talked about. Here, they thought they had a shoo-in to get first-hand information, and it didn't work. They must have been pissed off!

I started developing more of my own informants. This was driving the Meraz's crazy because one of the informants I developed was Enrique Medina's former sister-in-law, Martha Medina. She was the ex-wife of Juan Medina and provided a lot of information about the Jonases.

Martha asked me, "Do you know Peter Aduana?"

"I know the name."

Then she said, "I'm the one who provided him information on the Douglas tunnel in the late '80s."

Dianne DeMille PhD, Larry Hardin, Jeffrey Pearce, Randy Torgerson

Chapter 19: Taking FBI to San Luis, Mexico

1994

Several informants in the area told Larry that Enrique Medina, the manager at the maquiladora, had a lot of information on the computer in his office. The information includes the Asian's and Meraz's suspected heroin activities.

<><><>

Larry

I heard from the private investigators that they got a request from FBI Mark Spencer. "We'd like to set up a deal where we go into Mexico with you. And we want to go into Enrique's office at the maquiladora and download his computer." I was curious to know why Mark was now interested in reviewing Enrique's computer. Mark never gave me an explanation. I provided Mark with Enrique's Asian and Meraz connection.

This was highly unusual. In the 1990s the DEA could work in Mexico with their Federales under certain conditions. The FBI and United States investigators were not allowed to work in Mexico. It was illegal for the FBI to do this.

Jeff said, "Okay," to Mark. Jerry and Jeff were also willing to do it, but they wanted a copy of the information on Enrique's computer. Mark agreed.

I thought the connection between the Asians and Meraz's must be valuable since the FBI sent two agents to Enrique's office in San Luis, Mexico. Randy, Jeff, Javier Pina, and I all went to the border where we met FBI Agent Mark Spencer and a female agent from Washington DC. She identified herself as an information technology (IT) specialist. She just smiled when I asked her a question and would not communicate with me. I suspected she was working with the NSA or CIA.

Jeff didn't really like Mark Spencer and was wondering why the agent was so nice to him now. Agent Spencer was Mormon. He didn't drink beer or participate in dirty jokes. He never liked the private investigators.

◇◇◇

Jeff

I was directed to make this visit, and I was getting more nervous about going to Mexico because I knew I was becoming a target. The Meraz's knew who I was. I thought to myself, *Okay, this could be it for me! I don't know who these folks are, and I don't trust Mark.*

It was about 12:30 a.m., and four of us got into the car. Javier was driving, Jeff was in the front seat, and the two agents were in the back. Randy and Larry waited for them at the border. They drove across the border and over to the Grande Manufacturing building.

Javier said as he got out of the car, "Let me move security to the other side of the building. I'll be right back; just stay here." He moved security by asking them to check something in the back. Then he returned to get the others. The female agent/specialist had a laptop. She was quiet and unfriendly. Mark was carrying a notepad, and Jeff didn't have anything in his hands. Maybe she was sent to Mexico to see if the Asians were involved with the Meraz's.

We went into Enrique's office. The female agent started shoving floppy disks into the computer and typing away. I was watching the screen and could see The Blue Finn Seafood Company come up several times. She downloaded all this stuff to the floppy disks and kept saying, "This is good stuff! This is great! It's insane how much information is here on the Meraz's!" She was no longer quiet but excited.

I noticed a file cabinet and said to myself, *Well, I'm not going to stand here and do nothing.* I started going through all the files and saw a lot on The Blue Finn Seafood Company – their books, accounting, and communications. Loads of stuff!

I found a copier in the room and started copying whatever I could.

We spent about an hour and knew if we spent more than an hour, we were pushing our luck. The Federales would have shot us on the scene.

Javier said, "Okay, we gotta get outta here!"

As the specialist was putting everything back, she told Mark, "This is great shit!" She must have said it six or seven times!

We got back in the car and went across the border. Larry and Randy were waiting to meet us. The female agent said, "We're going to process this and get you a report."

I said, "And, don't forget, you're getting us a copy, too."

Everything changed that night. FBI Mark Spencer returned and told Larry he was going to get copies of everything from Enrique's computer. Mark now wanted to help Larry purchase 30 kilos of cocaine from Olegario using his CIs. Mark said he was going to work closely with Larry on the Meraz investigation, but Larry never got anything from him, and Larry never saw the female agent again or received the reports she had promised.

<><><>

Larry

Mark later refused to work with me on the Meraz investigation and refused to explain why he suddenly changed his mind about the 30 kilograms.

In intelligence, there are government-appointed people, elected people, and agents. There are witting and unwitting circumstances where some people know why they're doing something, and others don't. They were just told to do something, and they did it. Jeff thought the female specialist who got all the stuff from the computer was unwitting. She was told to get the information and that it was for something big. She didn't realize it was more of a cover-up type of action.

Nobody in Yuma liked Mark Spencer. When he was first put on the task force, he worked with me. He was kind of a jerk, not very cooperative. Some of that might have been DEA vs. FBI.

There was often a lot of friction back then. The relationship between DEA and FBI is better now.

Mark stopped communications with the private investigators and eventually with me. He never sent back anything to Jeff or me after we helped him get what he wanted from Enrique's office. Mark never gave me a reason why he didn't want to get involved in the Meraz case or with the Asians.

Jerry started blowing up FBI headquarters. "You guys went down there, risking my agents' lives. We want our copy of the report."

Several days later, Jerry contacted me about the information retrieved from Enrique's computer. I finally tracked Mark down at his office and said, "Dude, what's up? What happened? You were going to help me buy 30 kilos of cocaine from the Meraz brothers. What about the information you have on Enrique's computer?"

Mark responded, "Look, there's nothing there, and I can't tell you anything else. It's just a bunch of numbers." I knew someone higher up in the FBI must have stopped Mark working jointly in the investigation.

I met Jeff at Skyview and told him what Mark said.

Jeff told me, "I saw what was downloaded off Enrique's computer. Blue Finn Seafood Company! We have the copies I made from the files in the office. I gave them a copy and kept one for ourselves. It wasn't anything significant, but it did show shrimp loads, accounting, and communications. We even provided you a photo of Oswaldo meeting with Asians in El Golfo."

Jeff gave me a photo for my files. The photograph showed Oswaldo and Enrique with Asians at Oswaldo's store in El Gufo, Mexico. It was incredible to see them together.

It's clear to me that the Meraz's and Asians were running narcotics out of Grande. The private investigators quickly learned from this that if they gave anything to law enforcement, besides me, they needed to make copies, right then and there, for their own records.

Jeff was stealing their informants from other cops and flirting with their women. But Jeff was doing some damage. He had a better informant pool and contacts than a lot of law enforcement.

Norman sometimes worked undercover for the DEA and could get by as an illegal alien from Mexico. He followed Jeff and Randy when they were driving back to Fresno one Friday evening. They went through the agricultural stop on I-8, and they told the agricultural officer, "That dude behind us, he's illegal, stop him!" All Jeff could see in the rearview mirror was Larry's partner raising his middle finger. Larry was unaware that his partner was following the Pearce Investigators.

It got to the point where it was getting so "hot" with law enforcement looking for Jeff that he would go in and stay at the Shilo Inn one night and then the Holiday Inn the next. He moved around. He knew the desk clerks so well they would book him under another name. No one would ever know he was there.

Dianne DeMille PhD, Larry Hardin, Jeffrey Pearce, Randy Torgerson

Chapter 20: Jeff Gets More Involved

Indio, CA
1994, Jeff

Erik and I were driving 100 mph through Indio, on our way home to Fresno. Norman was following.

We saw a hubcap flying past us. Erik asked me, "What do you think?"

"I don't know. I think it's mine!"

This job was so intense, all the time. We had to be on our mark and watch everything.

I lost a marriage over this case. We got to a point where we were uncovering some crazy things, and I got in too deep. It was bad. I claimed it was the demise of my marriage mainly because I had a unique gift, which was my way of getting information.

It became a challenge to go to Yuma. I started sneaking in and out of town without being noticed! I would take a red-eye, started driving into town from Fresno, or I would come in at night. I wanted to keep the others guessing.

Larry had no clue that agents were following us. He knew things were getting over-the-top for me. He knew cops were trying to find a reason to get rid of me. The cops didn't do anything illegal, but they were doing a lot of things beyond what they should have been doing.

<><><>

Yuma, AZ
Randy

One week, Jeff and I drove into Yuma instead of flying, and when we finished on Friday, we drove home.

I was driving with Jeff in the passenger seat. As we came up to the agricultural checkpoint out of Yuma, a female California Highway Patrol officer pulled up and passed us.

I said, "Did you see her? She's beautiful!"

She was going about 70 mph. I pulled up beside her and looked over. She looked over at me and glared back. Then she flipped on her lights and came up behind to pull us over.

After we stopped, she came up to the car and asked me, "Do you realize how fast you were going?"

"I was going the speed limit, I thought!"

"No, you were going, 78."

I tapped on the speedometer and said, "Must be broken!"

"I need to see your license."

Then I leaned over and said, "Damn, you're beautiful!"

I was thinking: I'm going to get a ticket! Maybe I can get out of it.

She threw my license back at me and started laughing. "You guys have a nice day!" Then she walked back to her car and drove off.

We were lucky; she just laughed it off and let us go.

Chapter 21: Pedro Flies to Los Angeles

Yuma, AZ
1994, Larry

Oswaldo told Pedro the company that received his shrimp deliveries was called Blue Finn Seafood Company. Oswaldo and Enrique told Pedro about another shrimp business owner in Mexico, Mario Camaron, who also did business with Lan Bao Yang, an owner of Blue Finn Seafood Company.

I went back to my office and reviewed all my notes. I found many red flag targets by law enforcement showing that Blue Finn Seafood Company was suspected of moving white heroin into the United States. The Meraz brothers were involved with the Blue Finn Seafood Company. I asked myself, *Why are the Meraz brothers connected with Blue Finn Seafood Company? What's going on between the Meraz's and Blue Finn?*

I knew this was big! White heroin and Mexicans don't mix. The Meraz brothers have their black and brown heroin distribution in the United States. Something was not right here!

I got a message from Pedro that he was invited to Los Angeles with Oswaldo to visit Blue Finn Seafood Company and meet the owners.

I told Pedro, "We've got some activity going on between the Meraz brothers and Blue Finn. I wondered: *Why do the owners of Blue Finn want to meet with Pedro*?

"I think you should go with Oswaldo and learn as much as you can about the owners of Blue Finn. I want to know more about what's happening with Oswaldo and his friends in Los Angeles with their shrimp business," I said to Pedro.

Pedro got on a plane with Oswaldo at the Yuma International Airport, which I had under surveillance. When I saw them get on the flight, I contacted DEA Sam Little, who was the Asian Task Force case agent in Los Angeles, about the Meraz connection with

Blue Finn Seafood Company. The Pearce Investigators had given me Sam Little's name, and I already knew about Sam.

Sam's response was, "You're telling me a Mexican is coming over here with your source to meet the owners of Blue Finn? What's our surveillance?"

"Sam, I want you to protect my source if he needs it and gather information on the meeting with the Asians in Chinatown."

Sam wanted everybody in the Los Angeles Asian Narcotics Task Force to meet at the Los Angeles airport and follow Pedro and Oswaldo.

Sam said to me, "I'm going to come out to Yuma and see you when this is over."

Jeff was on his way home from Yuma for the weekend. He happened to be on the same flight to Los Angeles as Oswaldo, and then he would transfer to Fresno. Randy had gone home earlier. I didn't tell the Pearce Corporation anything about Pedro and Oswaldo.

Jeff was going berserk! Why was Oswaldo on this flight?

Before he got off the plane, Jeff decided to follow Oswaldo. He called Jerry and told him what was going on. He was going to see where he and the other guy (Pedro) were heading.

I got a call from Jerry Pearce. "What in the fuck are you doing? You should have told me the Meraz's were on the plane! I've got one of my guys, on that plane."

"Jerry, Jerry, calm down. The guy with Oswaldo is one of ours. He's a shadow." Jerry finally calmed down and stopped cursing.

Pedro and Oswaldo arrived at LAX, and Jeff was ready to follow. He saw Sam Little at the airport. He went to Sam and told him Oswaldo was on the plane. Sam already knew. He told Jeff he would drive, and they would follow the informant and the Meraz's. Since this was a DEA operation, Jeff had to take a later flight to Fresno. He missed his flight.

After Oswaldo and Pedro met with two Asian men at the airport, they went directly to Blue Finn Seafood Company in Los Angeles. Oswaldo introduced Pedro to the older Asian man. Pedro didn't get his name. They only shook hands and exchanged greetings.

The meeting didn't last long, and then the Asian employees took Pedro and Oswaldo back to the airport. Pedro told me nothing happened, and there had been no discussion of Pedro's shrimp business. Once in Yuma, Oswaldo never mentioned Blue Finn Seafood Company to Pedro again. After the meeting, I believe the Asian employees made eye contact with Sam Little. Pedro noticed Oswaldo's behavior toward him changed, and he wasn't sure what was happening.

I suspected the two Asian males might have observed Sam Little and his surveillance team following Pedro and Oswaldo from the LA airport to Chinatown. I sensed the Asians were aware that Pedro might be working with the government, even if they weren't sure which one.

Sam Little called and said it was highly unusual for Asians to meet with Mexican traffickers, could I come over to meet with him?

Sam kept questioning, "How did the Mexicans hook up with the Asian group?" I briefly filled him in that the private investigators named the Blue Finn Seafood Company and a meeting with Oswaldo Meraz.

In the next few days, I had a meeting with Sam Little near the courthouse in Los Angeles. It was very private and secure. Sam didn't talk a lot about the surveillance on Pedro and Oswaldo's meeting at Blue Finn Seafood Company. There wasn't even a written report on the surveillance. I knew something wasn't right when Sam didn't want to discuss Blue Finn. I asked Sam for further information about the company's connections with the CIA. Sam only appeared interested in leaving Los Angles and finding a position in China.

I decided to focus more attention on the Blue Finn Seafood Company. A couple of weeks later, I met with Sam in Los Angeles, and we went to Chinatown for dinner. Sam knew the Asian waiters and manager and spoke to them in their native language. Because of their connection to Chinatown where Sam lived, he wasn't interested in discussing Blue Finn Seafood Company. I didn't mention it to him again.

I learned that a DEA agent at the Consulate Office in Hermosillo and another agent out of Washington D.C. were working the Asian organization, especially Blue Finn Seafood Company.

I thought Sam Little didn't want to work on the Blue Finn case with me. He focused on himself and his career in Hong Kong or somewhere in China. Sam drove around with local PDs in the Los Angeles County area to gather intelligence in Chinatown. That's about all he did. He never talked about the targets in his group.

<>< ><>

Pedro and Enano again witnessed white heroin being put into tin foil bindles inside the tiger shrimp tails while sitting with Oswaldo at his business in El Golfo. The workers would filet the shrimp, cut out a pocket right in the middle of the tails, then put the tin folds inside, and close them up. The shrimp was loaded in kilo boxes that were iced and placed on racks. Then they loaded them into Oswaldo's refrigerator truck.

Pedro called me once he and Enano entered Arizona from Mexico and told me the white heroin was being moved soon to the states in an Oswaldo shrimp truck. Pedro provided me all the information I needed to stop Oswaldo's shrimp truck when it came across the border. I convinced my boss that we needed to search the shrimp truck.

My boss told me, "Larry if we don't find drugs this is going to cost us a lot of money because we're going to destroy all that shrimp."

146

"It's there. Pedro and Enano saw it with their own eyes!"

I was watching the Oswaldo shrimp truck enter the Arizona San Luis Port of Entry (POE) from Mexico. I knew it was loaded with drugs, and I was going to be the first agent to get the white heroin. I was excited that the Mexicans and Asians were smuggling white heroin into the U.S. *Wow!*

I was watching Oswaldo's shrimp trucks at the San Luis POE. The customs inspector opened the truck door. He walked in with his dog; he turned around and walked out. What was going on? Why didn't the dog alert to the drugs inside the truck?

Later, with agents from my office, I stopped the shrimp truck away from the San Luis POE. I had two border patrol agents I could trust with their drug-sniffing dogs to help locate the heroin inside the shrimp truck.

I thought I had tight control over who I could trust in border patrol, and no one was going to interfere in searching Oswaldo's shrimp truck. The agents' narcotic dogs alerted to the outside of the shrimp truck. I called for another dog from customs to smell any drugs on the shrimp truck. There was too much money being spent to break open the frozen shrimp boxes to not find dope. I had to make sure there were drugs inside the shrimp truck. If we didn't find anything, DEA would have to pay for the damage to the shrimp. Again, why didn't the inspector's dog alert at the Port of Entry in the shrimp boxes?

The other dog did the same thing and alerted me there was something on the shrimp truck. I told the driver to follow me to a cooling facility company in Yuma. When we arrived at the cooling center, the other agents and I took out slabs of five-kilo boxes of jumbo shrimp. The agents' dogs went crazy sniffing the suspected dope inside the boxes of shrimp. One of the dogs was taken around the slabs, and then he alerted to two particular ones. It was towards the back and in the middle of the shrimp truck.

Man, I got white heroin! I got it, guys! We finally made the case!

With the help of the other agents, we cracked the frozen boxes open and broke the shrimp tails. All the shrimp was lying there on the cooling floor. These beautiful, jumbo tiger shrimp, there was nothing inside the tails!

I'll be damned. Only a very few people knew about this. But someone leaked it to Oswaldo. The Meraz's or someone working at the San Luis point of entry switched the shrimp load on that truck in San Luis, Mexico so when it came across, there was nothing!

I could see it in their eyes, the border patrol agents, and the customs agents with their dogs. There was no dope! We were all surprised. The agents said to me, "Hey, we want this shrimp lying on the floor?"

I couldn't take the destroyed shrimp, so I let the border patrol and customs agents have it. Rumor has it, that night they had a nice barbecue feast.

I got a call from Pedro at the office telling me that load was going to the Blue Finn Seafood Company in Phoenix, not Los Angeles. Why did Oswaldo's shrimp truck suddenly change and move the shrimp to Phoenix, not Los Angeles? I couldn't prove it, but I was sure someone inside law enforcement, someone close to me, must have contacted Oswaldo.

The customs inspector at the point of entry called me, "Why did you stop that shrimp truck? I went in and out of that truck with my dog. I put some marijuana spray on the truck. I wanted to test my dog out."

Bullshit! How did the inspector know I was the one who stopped and searched the shrimp truck?

I asked him, "Why would you call and tell me that? Why did you target that shrimp truck to train your dog that day, and at that time?"

The customs inspector hung up on me.

I started to worry about Pedro and Enano's safety from corrupt law enforcement, not the Meraz brothers.

I got a call late that night from Oswaldo's wife, who said, "You destroyed my husband's shrimp."

"Ma'am! I'm going to hang up now." We destroyed a lot of shrimp, and she was giving me a hard time.

Later, I met Oswaldo's wife in Yuma. I told her she could contact DEA in Phoenix about the incident of her husband's shrimp truck. She said that I destroyed over $70,000 worth of shrimp. She added that she had seen me before in town and knew who I was. Without a doubt, the Commandanté's photo of me made it to the Meraz family.

I immediately said, "Why haven't I met you?"

Strangely, I never heard from Oswaldo about why his shrimp truck was stopped and shrimp destroyed. Oswaldo already knew the reason I searched his truck.

His wife was a very nice person, she went to the Catholic church, very connected with the Yuma community and yet her husband was having sex with young girls and moving drugs into the United States. Every year, she would get a brand-new Cadillac for Christmas with a big red ribbon from Johnny Perez, a car dealer in town. Johnny was a nasty guy, married to a gal from the post office. They were both very connected to the Meraz family.

A few days later, Pedro and Enano said they met with Oscar at Olegario's home. Oscar never mentioned the DEA searched Oswaldo's shrimp trucks. Even Oswaldo didn't mention his shrimp was destroyed. The DEA was obligated to pay out over $70,000 for that load of shrimp they destroyed. However, Oswaldo never asked them for the money.

The case was coming to an end. There were too many leaks with the few people I was working within the law enforcement community. I had tight control of it, but I never could figure out how the Meraz's knew what I was doing.

I found out later from a border agent at the INS Office of Personal Responsibility (OPR) in early 2001 that two agents were getting money under the table from narcotics traffickers in Mexico.

The agents were the dog handlers I used on Oswaldo's shrimp truck.

Pedro and Enano continued to meet with the Meraz brothers several times, but Oswaldo became less friendly with them than he had been before.

I kept wondering who was behind this. I could never put my finger on the guy who was leaking my information to other corrupt agents.

When Larry's informants were with Olegario and Oscar snorting coke up their noses, they listened to the brother's brag about their connections. They reported to me that the brothers talked about the CIA using the same routes as the Meraz's. Olegario made the statement, "I don't care what the DEA does, they'll never be able to touch me. I'm connected to the United States Government."

In July 1994, Pedro told me, "Oswaldo's wife said her husband is seriously addicted to drugs. Maria Solis [Oswaldo's mule and sex partner] told Pedro and Enano that Olegario and Oswaldo think we're DEA! We're getting worried. We don't want to go back and meet with any of them!"

According to Mario Camaron, the Meraz's were not only gatekeepers for narcotics, but they were also informants and assets for the Mexican government, in the same way as Blue Finn Seafood Company.

I thought That's why we were running into all these astronomical problems getting prosecutions.

I said later, "I'm the kind of guy who can put facts, evidence, and intelligence together for prosecution. You give me the bits and pieces, and I'll pull it together so the AUSA can prosecute. When the drug trafficking ties into something as big as Blue Finn and the Meraz brothers, I want to focus on the conspiracy to develop the drug trafficking connection. You might not get the guy hand-to-hand

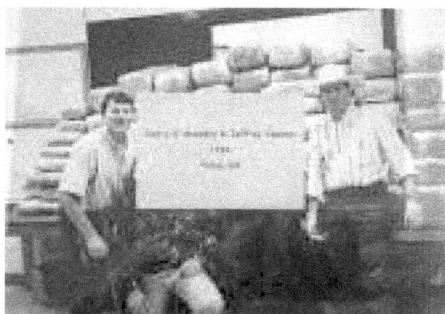
Larry R Hardin & Jeffrey Pearce
1994, Yuma AZ

undercover drug deal, but you've got to get the guy setting up the delivery."

I wanted to tell Jeff, Randy, Erik, and John so much over the years, but I couldn't because they weren't agents, they were private citizens. I commented to my wife, "I'm telling you; I feel very comfortable with these private investigators providing me information because they have my back and I have theirs. I'm constantly fighting battles, not only in my office, but also with the attorneys' office, and other agents in Yuma. When I'm close to arresting and prosecuting the Meraz brothers, I know these guys will keep me going!"

Private investigators usually had a team of people to support them. They couldn't believe I was only one DEA agent working the case. I was burning out. Jerry Pearce was continually coaching me. It was getting to the end, and enough was enough. Jerry started sending letters to me that were very encouraging. "Stay focused, man. You're doing this for the American public and the common good."

Dianne DeMille PhD, Larry Hardin, Jeffrey Pearce, Randy Torgerson

Chapter 22: A Meeting at the Icehouse; Yuma, AZ, and San Luis, Mexico

1994, Jeff

I was back in Yuma, and Javier Pina called me, "Hey, Jeff, there's some big meeting going on at the Icehouse."

"Okay."

I knew I needed to see what was happening, so I drove out and met Javier in San Luis by myself.

I grabbed my tape recorder and jumped into Javier's little Toyota truck. We drove across the border to the Icehouse with the recorder turned on. I started noting on my recorder California license plates as I saw them. There were probably 10-12 California plates at this meeting. *This couldn't be a meeting to buy shrimp. What could be so important? It must be about other cartel business.*

On our way back across the border, red lights flashed behind us. It was a black SUV with two Federales. It was getting serious!

I shoved the tape recorder up under the seat into the springs as hard as I could. They would kill me if they found it, no question about it. Everything would be over.

I told Javier, "You be cool, dude! You were taking me to Boys Town."

The two guys wore black outfits and machine guns around their necks. They walked up to our car. Javier got out of the truck. One started talking to Javier in Spanish, and the other guy came over and yanked me out of the truck. Then he went through the truck, pulling out everything he could find.

I was panicking, hoping he wouldn't find the recorder. The Federale kept saying, "You're La DEA. You're La DEA, La DEA!" pointing at me. I understood what he meant, but I acted like I didn't have a clue. The cop shoved the machine gun up to my mouth hard and kept repeating his claim that I was DEA. I was shaking like a leaf.

I finally said, "No, I'm not DEA. This is a friend of mine. He's taking me to Boys Town."

One of the guys spoke in broken English with Javier. Whatever Javier said, they turned to me and asked for my ID. I had a military reserve ID and showed it to them. There was an army base nearby, and I looked young enough that they bought it.

Apparently, we were spotted near the Meraz homes. Javier and I had made two passes through the area, and that made the Federales think we were up to something suspicious. Javier told them we were lost.

Finally, they said to Javier, "We're going to follow you to the border. Get your ass across it!"

Javier and I both got in the truck and started following the SUV. I was still shaking and thinking to myself: *I was this close to never seeing my family or my little girl ever again.*

The SUV stopped at the border, and Javier and I kept going.

When we crossed the border, I jumped out of the truck, dropped to the ground, and literally kissed it. I was so happy to be back in the United States. Larry had met Javier, but never trusted the guy. He told me, "When you do something like that by yourself, you've got to rely on somebody you can trust."

I later turned over the list of license plates to Larry and let him take it from there. I was so thankful I was spared and could still be with my family. I didn't want anything to do with going back down there to Mexico, ever again!

When I talked about it later, I told Larry, "I came close to death on a couple of occasions. I could have been killed!"

Larry told me that at one point, the Meraz's were thinking about putting a contract out on the Pearce Investigators. They didn't say my name, but the implication was me because I worked in Yuma all the time and was getting too close to their operations.

Larry talked about the danger I was in with because of my actions.

It was clear to me that I'd better get the hell out of town! I didn't come back for a very long time after that. It was getting gruesome!

<><><>

Larry

Jeff was taking way too much of a risk going into Mexico alone. As DEA, I might have done something like that, but I would have had protection. Javier could play both sides so easily. I didn't trust him.

Jeff had so much knowledge of the corruption. He was United States military and a United States Army Criminal Investigation Division (CID) agent. He was red-white-and-blue throughout! When he got involved with this case, he started seeing things that didn't make sense. This was law enforcement engaged in smuggling. He was involved up and down Nogales, Texas, Arizona, Arkansas, etc.

Jeff responded, "This was the breaking point for me. I was really under pressure. My life at home was falling apart. My wife was seeing a neighbor across the street, in Fresno. I was a young man and honing my skills on the job."

He had a knack for getting people to confess. Jeff explained, "They sent me to Texas to interview a guy who worked at the cold-storage facility. It took me seven hours, but he confessed! And he told me how the laundering operation worked."

He could get any information he needed, especially from women. I knew Jeff was moving too fast with the girls. He was a young guy, good looking, and he got carried away. He got involved with the wives and girlfriends of other cops and informants. That's where he started having problems.

I was concerned about him because if he'd been DEA or a cop, he would have lost his job long ago. He got too close to the dark side. He worked so hard that he started losing sight of the big picture, putting the Meraz brothers in jail. I told him I couldn't bring him back; he had to watch himself because he was dealing with the Blue Finn Seafood Company, and they were really bad news.

When Norman was doing surveillance down in San Luis, Mexico, I stayed behind on the United States border because my Spanish wasn't the best. I was providing him with security on this side of the border in case something happened in Mexico. According to Larry, Norman got pulled over by local Mexican police. They found his badge because he was traveling around the Meraz neighborhood. The Mexican police kicked and punched him in the kidneys. He was hurting. He had tears in his eyes when he came back across the border into the U.S.

There were several times when Lieutenant Danny Elkins of the Southwest Narcotics Task Force would go down to the Mexican border with me. We worked well together. We had the same goal. Danny wanted to put the Meraz brothers in jail as much as I did. Danny couldn't believe the Asians were involved with the Meraz brothers.

I told the private investigators, "It's not safe for any of you to go down to Mexico. If the Meraz's thought Jeff was DEA – it's hard to say where he'd be now."

Things were getting out of control. Jeff was pushing the envelope too fast in his desire to end the investigation. He was leading a life that was on the edge, that I called the dark side, El Camino del Diablo. He had a relationship, a wife, and a kid and yet, he got caught up and started taking chances that crossed the line.

Kiki Camerena trusted the local Mexican cops, and that trust cost him his life. It was corruption plain and simple. Law enforcement found him and helped torture him to death. His Mexican cop buddies were the ones who know he'd been tortured.[90]

Jeff was so involved that I was getting calls from other DEA agents and police officers in El Centro and Calexico about the Pearce Corporation, "Who are these Pearce Investigators?"

I enjoyed working with the private investigators because I felt comfortable. I really did. I never felt that way with the agents and cops in the community. Some agents and cops didn't like the private investigators.

One night when Jeff was at a party, he met a drunk woman bragging about her husband being a DEA agent. He was flirting with her but decided to call me before going further. "Is this gal the wife of an agent?"

I told him, "Yes, leave her alone. You don't want to get involved with her! Don't want to dance with the devil. The grace of God has got you here for a reason. Don't let the devil play with your mind, Jeff. The devil plays with your soul."

Today, I say to my students, where did the evil thoughts come from? Those thoughts that suddenly pop into your mind? They're evil! I'm giving you advice from the tree of knowledge. It's yours to take."

Dianne DeMille PhD, Larry Hardin, Jeffrey Pearce, Randy Torgerson

Chapter 23: A Set-up

Yuma, AZ
1995, Jeff

It was late at night. Erik Hansen and I had been drinking for several hours. When we got back to the Best Western hotel, I went straight to bed. My pager went off at 2:00 a.m. It was from Fernando, my CI. I called him back, "I have an undercover tape that I want to get to you. It's between Enrique and me on negotiating a heroin buy."

"Okay, where are you?"

"I'm in the lobby."

I was Fernando's primary contact. I never specifically let him know where I was staying, only that I was in town. How did he know where I was? How did he end up in the lobby of the hotel where I was staying? Where did he get that information?

I grabbed a pad and pen on my way out the door and went downstairs. I was barefoot and wore a pair of shorts and a t-shirt. There was a very attractive girl standing at the main entrance to the lobby.

She said, "Hey, watch out; there's some glass there!"

I looked down and saw the glass, "I appreciate that. Thanks!"

I went to the other side of the lobby to meet Fernando. He gave me the tape, and I took notes on what he had to say.

As I was heading back to the elevator, the girl asked me, "Why are you up so late? Or is it early?"

"Work," I told her Then we started talking. Some touchy, feely stuff went on.

Then I told her, "I gotta go, I gotta go to bed."

"Well, I'm waiting for my boyfriend," she said.

"Okay, Good night!"

When I came down to the desk to check out the next morning, the desk clerk told me, "Hey, law enforcement was here last night and asked some questions about you."

"So, what's new?"

I didn't think anything of it. I got on the plane and went back to Fresno. Two weeks later, Erik and I went back to Yuma. It was in September, dove hunting season. We took our shotguns so we could go dove hunting with Jack Pollard one afternoon while we were in town.

When we got to the hotel, a car pulled up, and two detectives approached me. One was Nilsson, a narcotics cop, and the other was Schneider, who worked sexual assaults.

"We want you to come down and talk with us," Nilsson said.

"About what?"

"It's confidential, and you probably don't want to talk about it here."

"I don't give a shit! What is it?"

"There's been some allegations that you sexually assaulted a female guest here at the hotel last week."

"What? I didn't sexually assault anybody."

"Well, come on down, and we'll talk about it."

So I got in the patrol car, no cuffs or anything. It was obvious I didn't have a choice. They took me down to the station and into a room with both of them.

I asked Nilsson, "Why are you here?" He's been targeting me, but he's narcotics.

"Uh, we were short on manpower."

"Short on manpower? So, they call a narcotics officer out? That's bullshit!"

I told them I remembered the situation and explained what happened. Then I said, "I didn't force anything, I'll take a polygraph, whatever you want me to do!"

"Well, we're going to arrest you."

They put my ass in the Yuma County jail on $50,000 bond. I called my wife and said, "Just move on." She was going to find out everything, it was going to come out, and she wasn't going to

160

want to be with me anymore. We already had difficulties, and I knew this was going to be her breaking point.

They put what I said to her in the report, but they said I confessed to her on the phone.

I said to them, "I didn't confess to shit!"

I got bonded out, stayed in the hotel, and took a plane back the following morning. Rolf picked me up from the airport. At that point, I thought my life was over. I had never been arrested in my entire life. Ever! I have Top Secret/Sensitive Compartmented Information clearance, etc. I may have been messing around, but I'm a good guy! The reason I worked so hard was that I wanted to see an end to drug trafficking and corruption. Was I just set up by Fernando? I'm not sure how he knew where I was staying. I figured he must have been helping them.

I paid $5,000 for an attorney and went for my preliminary hearing. Back then, the victim had to testify, and she was a no-show. The girls' parents were also trying to sue the hotel for not providing security for the girl. The case against me was dismissed with prejudice. Meaning it could be refiled.

The District Attorney at that time, a nice guy said to me, "I want you to know Jeff; I didn't refile this case. It was Nilsson!"

In Yuma, it didn't take a District Attorney to file; a cop could file a case. Detective Nilsson went down and refiled! This was out of line!

I had a good reputation with a lot of law enforcement in the area, and they knew I was a stand-up guy. There was just this one little group who didn't like me.

I showed up again for the hearing, and when I went in, Schneider and Nilsson were sitting there waiting for me.

It was the same judge as the last time. He asked, "Where's the victim?"

"We can't find her, your honor."

"Did you subpoena her?"

"Yep!"

"No kidding! Didn't show, huh?"

He turned to me and said, "Mr. Pearce, I apologize for Yuma County wasting your time and trying to convict you of something that is obviously not your doing!"

The prosecutor got up and said, "I would like to apologize to Mr. Pearce formally."

When I walked by Schneider and Nilsson, it took everything I had not to give them the finger. I said quietly, "Fuck you for doing this to me!"

I now have an arrest record for sexual assault, and I've had to answer for that over the years. When I applied for my private investigator license in 1997, they brought up my full record, and I had to explain what happened. And I had difficulties when I got my firearm. They brought it up then, too. To this day, it follows me. It never drops off the radar!

<><><>

Fresno, CA
Jeff

Because of this incident, I was benched by Jerry and not allowed to leave Fresno. I started working on a link analysis chart for the case on my laptop. I pulled binder after binder off the shelf and started refreshing my memory of the details related to the case. I created the chart and taped the pieces together. It stretched out to about 8-feet wide with 12-point font. Then I took the pieces, section by section, to a blueprint copy machine and put the whole chart together. It took me about three to four months to complete.

Jerry thought I wasn't doing much in the office until one day he saw the chart. Jerry told me to keep it up. There were more than 200 binders in the office I used to create the link analysis chart. I did most of the work myself. The other investigators would take turns adding information, and the chart grew.

John took my place in Yuma. Then Jerry realized that was a waste of time because no one would talk to him. I had developed my informants, and they don't just start talking with anyone.

162

Informants are only as good as the investigator using them. When you pay an informant, it's like feeding a stray dog. Soon that dog will only come to you. Jerry wanted to send me back again because John was too laid back, and he didn't have the personality to get the work done. It was almost like he was afraid, and he didn't have the network I had established. My informants were not real friendly to John or anyone else. That's the nature of informants.

I was still shaken up. It got to me. My wife filed for divorce, and I was going through a custody battle for my three-year-old daughter. I didn't want to see Yuma again. I was struggling with the decision to return. Part of me wanted to, but part of me didn't.

I described it as the most traumatic experience of my entire life. To this date, I can deal with almost anything, but because of who I am, being accused of such a heinous crime was very difficult to live with. I would describe it as, feeling like somebody dumped dog shit on me and I couldn't clean it off.

<><><>

In this case, there were several law enforcement agencies involved in some way. They wouldn't talk to each other. As the case went on, we developed friendships with many of the people we were dealing with. We became liaisons between law enforcement agencies.

We did lots of surveillance at Blue Finn Seafood Company and suspected heroin was arriving in large quantities.

We needed more information about the shipments going to Blue Finn Seafood Company. Randy and John went to Terminal Island and talked with a U.S. Customs agent who dealt with shipping. The agent told them that twice a year a shipment of 600 pounds of white heroin was going to the Blue Finn Seafood Company and United States Customs Agents were told not to do anything about it. They were told it was going to be intercepted at another time as part of a larger operation. Then the agent said, "I never got any memos that something came of these shipments. Every time we were told the same thing."

So, that was 1,200 pounds of white heroin a year! That confirmed the Blue Finn Seafood Company-Chinese connection.

Chapter 24: Buying A Sample; Yuma, AZ

1994, Larry

On the day to purchase the one-kilo sample of cocaine, Pedro was in jail for a DUI, so Enano showed up in Yuma to help make the sample buy. I had to negotiate this deal using my friend's help.

I didn't speak Spanish fluently, so I told my friend, "You come with me. I need you to talk to Enano."

I drove my personal vehicle, a little green 1990 Mazda. We went to meet with Enano behind the grocery store, but he didn't show up. So, I called him and explained to my friend that my source from Colombia, was going to talk with him.

My friend told Enano in Spanish, "Don't be a sissy. Set up the purchase for the sample kilo with José Jonas Rodriguez." Enano didn't have the cajones to make a deal with José. He was just a bodyguard, and Pedro was in jail.

Enano wasn't comfortable making the buy without Pedro. He trusted Pedro. He wanted to talk with him before making the buy.

Pedro talked with Enano on the phone from jail, "You need to talk to this girl because she's behind the deal."

Enano listened to my friend and attempted to make the buy.

José finally said, "Okay, I'll deliver the kilo of coke in Phoenix."

Enano set it up. I said to Agent José, "We're going to Phoenix, we've got a kilo of coke waiting! You'll be meeting with José Jonas Rodriguez at Denny's." José couldn't buy anything as an agent, and he was not too sure about this buy.

I had information from Pedro and Enano that Olegario and Oscar Meraz were ready to sell them 30 kilos of coke for $14,500 a kilo. I needed to purchase a one-kilo sample before making the full buy to make sure it was the real deal because that was a lot of money to pay.

I bought the sample kilo of coke through Enano. I field-tested the white power substance, and everything appeared to be authentic. Pedro and Enano set up the rest of the buy when I was ready with the money.

AUSA Richard Dreamer wanted to meet with Pedro and Enano. I arranged the meeting. Pedro, Enano, and I met with Dreamer at his office in Phoenix, Arizona. Both sources were dressed in suits and didn't look like they were criminals working for DEA. I had told them to look professional because they were going to go into the Grand Jury or would be testifying at the hearing. They looked and smelled good. Pedro was a very classy individual and always looked good. He owned his own business and did very well. He just had a bad habit with girls and snorting coke.

Pedro and Enano told Dreamer the details, and he started to back off. Richard didn't want to indict the Meraz's, but only charge the mules, the low-level people.

Dreamer said, "You don't have enough to prosecute Olegario or Oswaldo for conspiracy to transport narcotics into the United States nor their statements of trying to kill Don and Roy in 1975. Oscar is a possibility for a federal indictment."

I was thinking to myself: He only wants to indict the mules, maybe Oscar. He can't do that! They bought a kilo of coke and Olegario set it up with Pedro to buy 30 kilos!

"How about Oswaldo and his relationship with Blue Finn Seafood Company?" Pedro asked.

Richard looked as if he hadn't heard the name of Blue Finn Seafood Company. He asked Pedro and Enano, "How were you so successful to penetrate the Meraz family?"

During Richard Dreamer's meeting, I found out Pedro did coke at the Grande business with Enrique and the Meraz brothers. I had no idea Pedro and Enano were doing drugs with the Meraz's in Mexico, and I especially didn't like them having sex with young girls. The brothers were having sex with girls who were 12 and 13 years old. But Pedro and Enano were definitely part of the Meraz

166

group. AUSA Dreamer was freaking out that the sources were snorting drugs in Mexico.

Pedro remarked, "We had to snort coke and have sex with numerous young women whenever we met with the Meraz brothers. The brothers know agents and law enforcement can't do drugs or have sex with young girls. Only bad law enforcement."

I told Dreamer immediately, "I never instructed them to use coke, only to stay alive." Then I said to him, "Damn it, Richard, it takes a crook to do a crook."

Dreamer said, "I can't do this. I can't prosecute the case."

I was thinking: He's sabotaging the case.

I yelled, "This is bullshit!"

Pedro looked directly at Dreamer and told him, "Why did I go to prison for five years for helping an undercover agent to buy some cocaine? I was charged with conspiracy and never saw the coke. Look at all I did for this case! I called my friend that I buy coke from and told him I want you to meet this guy because he wants to buy some of your stuff. He's ready to deal!"

That wasn't good, Pedro talking to Dreamer like that.

I looked at Dreamer and said, "You son of a bitch! You can't do that. You've got the Meraz's, all over this. The brothers already talked to Pedro and Enano about the involvement in the attempted killing of the DEA agents. It's on the recordings. This is a conspiracy! At least let me pick them up. You can get them with the Grand Jury. You can indict anyone on a Grand Jury. Let me bring them in and start squeezing them. Separate them, find out what's going on here. When they do that, it'll shut down their whole organization."

Dreamer's response was, "I can't prosecute this case."

I looked at Pedro and Enano and told them, "Let's get the hell out of here! This son-of-bitch is not going to prosecute Olegario or even Oswaldo. You should never have mentioned Blue Finn Seafood Company."

Pedro looked at me strangely, and when we walked out of Dreamer's office. I said, "I'm gonna lose my job. You can't talk like that to an Assistant United States Attorney. They've got so much clout, so much power, all our authority from DEA has dwindled."

Pedro and Enano were extremely upset because they thought Dreamer was looking for an easy excuse to get out of indicting Olegario, Oscar, and Oswaldo.

The sources had put their butts out there. I was thinking about how the sources were following my instruction to target the Meraz brothers; *These Meraz guys knew what we were doing. But then you have an AUSA who tells you something like that! It just isn't right! I understand why Pedro and Enano don't trust the agents in my office anymore nor the United States Attorney's Office, after meeting with AUSA Richard Dreamer.*

Remember, it takes a criminal to do a criminal.

After the meeting with Richard Dreamer, the whole Meraz case started to disappear. Pedro and Enano were still around, but they didn't want to work with me again. They didn't want anything to do with the case. All because once again, the Blue Finn Seafood Company was involved. The AUSA didn't have the guts to prosecute the brothers.

Richard Dreamer was still around, prosecuting low-level cases but never worked again on the Meraz case. He didn't want anything to do with it.

<><><>

I got a call from Phoenix, "You've got a new AUSA, his name is Jimmie Lost." He was a real young guy, very naïve and very liberal to the left when it comes to prosecuting narcotics. He thought the federal drug charges were too harsh.

Every time I got a new United States Attorney involved, they would come to Yuma. I would take them into Mexico and show the Meraz miniature size white houses, and then, of course, the AUSA would get excited about the case. There was plenty of information to indict Enrique.

168

Like Dreamer, I invited Jimmie Lost down to Yuma, and across the border to see the Meraz homes. I wanted him to have a clear visual picture of what I was talking about; the miniature white houses with marble pillars imported from Italy. The owner was Olegario, a produce farmer, and yet, he wasn't producing much produce. The other house was owned by Oswaldo, who was providing shrimp to Blue Finn Seafood Company.

As it turned out, Lost didn't understand why charges were so severe for cocaine trafficking. Federal laws were that way; the states played it their own way. In Miami, a kilo of coke would get a lesser charge than in Kentucky. San Diego is off the market. The new AUSA didn't want anything to do with the Meraz's. He just wanted the mules. I didn't want to let the Meraz's get off so easy.

<>>

Later, Sam Little called me and said he was coming out to Yuma with an agent out of DEA headquarters in Washington D.C. The agent was assigned to work with Asian groups and was working with Sam Little on the Intel part in Los Angeles. He wanted to discuss the Blue Finn Seafood Company and the Meraz's.

Jimmie Lost was also there when I presented the case showing the direct evidence that tied in with the Blue Finn Seafood Company meetings with the Meraz's. They all said it was prosecutable. I thought the DEA guy working with Jimmie Lost was there to protect the Blue Finn Seafood Company. I could tell Jimmie just came down for one reason; to see what we were going to share at the meeting, but not to do anything.

I couldn't understand that. This was my last pitch to try to indict them. If we could get the Meraz's, then we were going to find out who this Asian organization was and what they're all about. Sam Little didn't provide anything. He was strictly an intelligence guy. He knew a lot about Blue Finn Seafood Company but wasn't going to tell me anything. That was my last meeting with Sam Little and the agent from Washington, D.C. Jeff and Randy couldn't sit in, but they were around outside the meeting.

That night, after the meeting, I brought Jimmie to Johnny's Sports Bar, where he was meeting Jeff and Erik. We were all drinking a few beers. Jeff got to talking with AUSA Jimmie Lost and got into an altercation. Jimmy and Jeff got plowed and were feeling no pain.

Jeff shouted, "You should indict them!"

Jimmie said he was not going to indict.

Jeff was ready to go into blows with this guy.

Jeff told Jimmie, "You know; you should indict these guys. Larry has all the information you need. It's all there for you."

"I don't have enough to prosecute Enrique Medina," Jimmie said.

Jeff was getting upset, "I know you have more than enough."

"Are you threatening a United States Attorney?"

I told them, "Come on, you guys, come on, come on. Let's get out of here!"

Jeff said, "You motherfucker!"

"Yeah," Jimmie said, "You haven't seen your day, yet!"

Yuma was not a place for this to happen. Especially with the Blue Finn Seafood Company and the growing Hispanic community connections.

Chapter 25: Everything Sent to DEA Council Yuma, AZ

1995, Larry

In 1995, I sent everything I had to Washington D.C. DEA Chief Counsel. I received a response from Chief Counsel, "We've reviewed the case. Great job. You have the evidence. Just get it prosecuted!" I was excited to get this done and planned to meet with Lieutenant Danny Elkins. I wanted to show him the letter from Washington D.C. to the Yuma County Attorney's Drug Task Force office.

◇◇◇

Larry R Hardin 10-26-1995
32 Kilos Cocaine

I met with Lieutenant Danny Elkins to see if he would help me prosecute the Meraz brothers in Yuma County. I gave Danny the case file to review the evidence and DEA Chief Counsel statements. After one day, Danny called me and yelled, "You've got them, Larry!"

Danny was so excited to have a case against the Meraz's. He said, "The county attorney's office will indict the brothers in Yuma."

Danny couldn't understand why the AUSA Office in Phoenix didn't want to prosecute this case. He told me, "I want you to talk to the County Prosecutor, Joanne Green, here in Yuma. She's in charge of the narcotics unit. I've already called Joanne about your case. She's as excited as I am that the Meraz brothers are going be charged for their crimes."

The next day, Danny and I met with Yuma County Attorney Joanne Green. Green knew the Meraz brothers and their criminal activities. She was aware of how dangerous it was working so closely to the border. I presented her with the case review from DEA Chief Counsel. She was speechless when she read the Chief Counsel recommended the case should be submitted to a Grand Jury.

After our long meeting, she was excited to assign the case to one of her young, new attorneys to present to a Grand Jury. I told her, "I'm ready now to meet in front of the Grand Jury."

The young attorney was from the East Coast. He was a clean-cut guy and was freaking out because he really wanted this case. This would be a big feather in his cap. Based on the evidence, Green was sure the Grand Jury would indict the Meraz brothers on State charges.

I continued to meet with Lieutenant Elkins to talk about how we could work together on the Meraz case.

◇◇◇

Soon after, Leonardo told me, "Larry, you need to talk to Officer Tom Diaz about the Meraz case. He's been assigned to help on your investigation. We've got to bring Tom on board because he's going to be working the border in San Luis."

When I met Diaz, I explained the Meraz investigation. I was thinking to myself: I don't know this guy, is he corrupted? Why is Leonardo pushing me to work with him?

Larry R Hardin 1995
10 lb. brick Marijuana of
Meraz produce truck

I gathered all the evidence, notes, everything, and a copy of the Meraz investigation letter from Washington, DC, and the review from DEA Chief Counsel. The DOJ/DEA Chief Counsel had reviewed the case, laying out the Federal charges and the indictment against each Meraz brother. I knew I had the evidence against the Meraz brothers. The Chief Counsel had prepared the case for AUSA Jimmie Lost to prosecute. AUSA Lost refused to prosecute the

172

brothers, as he put it, due to lack of evidence. The brothers bragged to the sources about trying to kill the agents. The sources recorded the brothers boasting. But Lost didn't care.

Later, I told the Chief Counsel, "It's the same evidence I gave to both AUSAs Richard Dreamer and Jimmie Lost."

Chief Counsel knew, without a doubt, that I had what I needed to prove the case because I had some great information from working with the private investigators. The case was already prepared! It was ready for the Federal Grand Jury, based on the evidence and information provided.

Larry R Hardin 1995
Larry R Hardin
Burning Marijuana from

Larry R Hardin
Cocaine 1995

AUSA Chief Legal Counsel in Washington D.C. said to me, "Larry, the case is already done – whoever gets it, they don't need to do anything! It's ready to go! It's all written out, and you've got the evidence to back it up."

They added, "You need to indict these people with all the evidence."

I responded, "I want to do this for Don and Roy."

I'm going to give this case to the Yuma County Attorney's office.

Later, Lost asked me to meet him at his office in Phoenix.

Lost told me, "We can indict José Jonas Rodriguez for the sale of the kilo of cocaine to the undercover agent, but nothing else."

I told him, "I'm going to take this case to the county prosecutor. They want to process it and indict these brothers!"

Lost said, "Larry, you can't take this case; it's a federal investigation."

I told him, "You're wrong, buddy. I'm going to take it to the county because they're going to do it. They're going to indict everybody on that list." Then I yelled, "The Meraz's tried to kill two DEA agents. That's a no-no. You don't get to do that! That's part of my family." This was a big letdown!

The meeting ended without agreeing to indict the Meraz brothers. It would be the last meeting I had with Napolitano's attorneys.

As I was walking out, I was thinking to myself: Why, does Jimmie only want a mule, when everything's documented, and it becomes discovery?

I walked out of Lost's office again and returned to the Yuma Office.

I was thinking: Nothing's going to happen with this case! I'm not going anywhere with the Meraz's. I'll never get them because Jimmie said I don't have enough evidence right now. Is the CIA involved in this investigation?

Lost told me, "It won't happen!"

But I had a strong belief that I was going to get the Meraz brothers for attempting to kill Don and Roy.

◇◇◇

That night, when I was driving back to the office from meeting with Jimmie Lost in Phoenix, I decided I would continue with my meeting with Joanne Green and the new attorney the following day. I was ready to tell them, "The case is finally yours."

While driving, I got a message that Leonardo wanted to talk to me. Rather than heading home, I went straight into the office to see him.

I just wanted to make a quick stop and then go home to rest. When I walked in, Leonardo called me to his office. There he was sitting behind his big oak desk with Joanne Green and the new prosecutor in front of him. I was wondering *What's going on? Aren't we supposed to meet in the morning?*

I said, "You know Joanne, I have been working the Meraz case for several years."

Leonardo said, "Larry, you need to sit down." I wondered if this was about the meeting with AUSA Jimmie Lost in Phoenix? "No, I'm going to stand up," I said. I had just been driving for three-and-a-half-hours from Phoenix.

Leonardo said, "Officer Tom Diaz went to Joanne."

Joanne said, "Yeah, Tom Diaz came to our office and said there would be threats against us because we were targeting the Meraz family."

I thought to myself, Tom Diaz went to the Yuma attorney's office, behind my back, behind everyone's back, and told Joanne Green "If you take this case, there's a chance you and your new attorney will get killed." Tom Diaz scared the hell out of them! The reason Tom scared them was that he knows the Meraz's. Wow, Tom Diaz is one of the corrupt cops.

I told the attorneys, "Tom is either corrupt or crazy."

Leonardo said he would contact the FBI and report Tom's threat to the attorneys.

The new attorney, nervously said, "Larry, I have a family."

So, the case went downhill from there.

Randy later said, "I believe it's not the criminals that threatened Joanne Green. I think it was FBI that put Tom Diaz up to threatening her."

FBI interviewed Officer Tom Diaz for corruption and threatening the county attorneys. The FBI reported to Leonardo, "You know what, we can't do anything with Officer Diaz. He's kind of mentally deranged."

When I heard that, I said to Leonardo, "Yes, but corrupt, too. He's mentally sick. You wanted him to work with me on the Meraz case. That's bullshit, and you know it."

I was thinking: What? Officer Tom Diaz threatens the attorneys for working the Meraz case? And Leonardo isn't going to do anything about it?

These were the FBI agents from Phoenix. FBI made it go away by protecting Officer Diaz.

Somebody is always behind the scenes on me. I'm surprised I didn't get killed, but if I did, DEA would go crazy, my family would go crazy to find the person. I'm amazed Randy and Jeff, weren't whacked, either.

I told my wife, "It's time for me to go. The Meraz case is over!"

I already bought a kilo of coke, and the ASUA in Phoenix would only indict one mule, José Jonas-Rodriguez, Meraz's right-hand man. José was a close associate of the Meraz's and was always at the meetings with Oswaldo, Oscar, and Olegario when Pedro and Enano were there.

This was so sad when I look back on it because I did a lot of work. I feel like I didn't do Don and Roy justice. I felt disgraced because I didn't get the Meraz brothers.

I had no one working with me on this case at the office, except these private investigators. Some of the agents and cops wanted to stay away from the private investigators. I felt like I was by myself.

According to my sources and informants, Officer Tom Diaz was corrupt. I couldn't prove it, but I had to be cautious. I warned the agents in my office to stay away from Diaz, "You don't want to fool with Diaz, he's corrupted."

◇◇◇

I was with a group of agents, waiting for a load of dope to come across. We were all driving pick-up trucks. New DEA Supervisor Leonardo Castillo came out to meet with us in the desert in his Mercedes sedan.

He wanted to tell me what I should and should not do. I was a senior guy, running the Yuma office for several years, and I knew what I was doing.

I always carried a backup gun in my ankle holster, a snub-nose five-shot revolver .38 Special. A .38-revolver saved Don and Roy from being killed by the Meraz's. I looked at Castillo and said, "You know Leonardo, I can take this .38 from my ankle holster, I can sit here and play with it, and you know what? I might just drop this thing, and a round could go off and hit you in the damn leg, you know that?"

He looked at me. I looked at him and laughed. Castillo smiled nervously and got in his car and left. He probably thought I was crazy. I wasn't going to shoot anybody. I was trying to get him to leave me alone. Let me do my job because I was dealing with a group of people here who were dangerous.

Castillo got involved, especially when Officer Tom Diaz made a threat. He was worried about me.

Dianne DeMille PhD, Larry Hardin, Jeffrey Pearce, Randy Torgerson

Chapter 26: Shooting of Elkins and Crowe; Yuma, AZ

1995

Southwest Border Alliance Drug Enforcement Task Force included United States Customs, state troopers, border patrol agents, deputy sheriffs, cops, and other local law enforcement agencies. DEA, FBI, and IRS are not located within the alliance. The alliance group of about 22 members investigated drug activities in the Yuma area, where Arizona, California, and Mexico meet.[91] They stored their evidence in the evidence locker in their building.[92]

<><><>

Larry

Lieutenant Danny Elkins was so excited that he would be helping me to get the Meraz brothers indicted with the local prosecutor's office in Yuma, Arizona. Just a few days later, before the 4th of July, San Luis, Arizona Police Officer Tom Diaz threatened the County Prosecutor if they indict the brothers for drug state violations.

Regularly, I ran along the water canal to reduce office stress from working long hours. On the early morning of July 5, 1995 (my birthday), a United States Marshal rode his bicycle up to me saying, "Last night Danny Elkins and Mike Crowe were killed at their office by Jack Hutchinson." Danny was a Yuma PD lieutenant, Mike was with the Department of Public Safety (DPS), and Jack was a Yuma County deputy sheriff officer.

I went to the crime scene in the evidence locker, but they wouldn't let me in. I talked with James, the custodian of evidence who survived the shoot-out.

Lieutenant Danny Elkins was married with a son and daughter. He was also a member of and in charge of the Organized Crime Drug Enforcement Narcotics Task Force. He knew someone inside the group was stealing drugs and other things from the evidence locker, so he installed a video camera in the evidence vault.

Lieutenant Elkins had just come back from a fishing trip with his son on July 4. James Ehrhart, a retired DPS officer and the custodian of evidence, was at the evidence locker and looked at the video and then called an agent, Jerry Mason, "I got the person identified. You can see him going into the evidence vault. It's Jack!"

He said to Jerry, "Stay put. I want to call Elkins. We're coming over, and we're going to talk about this. We've got to do something about it now because everybody's out for the Fourth of July watching the fireworks at the Marine Corps Base."

Jack was a retired staff sergeant in the Marine Corps. They knew Jack was involved with the missing evidence, but they didn't realize everything connected to it.

After making the call, Jerry and James went over to the parking lot and drove to the back where the agents enter the building.

The building was shaped like a box with windows only at the front entrance. This was how they conserved energy. Several agents worked in the back of the building, where they would park. From the front entrance, you could only get back there through one long narrow hallway. There was no other way out of the building.

It was very secure with wire fencing all the way around. In the front, there was another parking area with a dumpster. The public went in and out at the front. Everyone who worked there had weapons, but when it got hot, most of them would leave their weapons in their cars and trucks while they were in the building.

After reviewing the video, they called the sergeant from DPS, Michael Crowe.

When Danny got there, He and Jerry reviewed the video evidence with James. They noticed Mike was already there and Jack Hutchinson's car was in the parking lot out back.[93, 94]

Jack had long hair and wore a bandanna, black pants, a black shirt, and was carrying bolt cutters. They saw Jack right away as he
180

looked up at the ceiling. They were sure he noticed the camera. He was walking down the narrow hallway as Mike approached him. Jack turned around and walked outside. While he walked out, Danny, James, and Jerry thought he was leaving the building because he knew he was caught or maybe he was trying to do something to make it look like somebody else had been stealing evidence.

Then, Jack came back in the door and started shooting. His gun jammed. Danny and Jerry ran down the hallway and into the bay. There was no way in or out. James was still in the hallway and stood his ground as Jack approached him. Jack had the eyes of Manson: dead, nothing there. He pointed the weapon straight at James. Click, click. He was out of ammunition. James watched Jack go down the hallway and out to his car. Danny and Jerry ran out to the hallway to see if James was okay. James yelled, "Let's go out the front door."

As James ran out the front, he heard more shooting inside. He jumped behind the dumpster. He looked up and saw Mike coming around the building, running. Behind him was Jack, shooting at him.

Mike, for some reason, tried to crawl under a car, a Jeep Cherokee that had been left there all night in the public parking lot. Jack grabbed him by his feet, pulled him out, and shot him. As Jack walked away, Danny had come into the front reception area and got on the phone to call Yuma PD for help.

It's like going hunting; you never know if you've killed your animal until you put a round in his skull. Mike wasn't dead. Jack walked away, and then Mike scooted up behind him just sitting on his butt. He was crying. He had just given Jack an "outstanding" on his report. Jack came over and shot him again.

With Mike was lying on the ground, Jack went back inside.

The partitions inside are low. They could see most of what happened from the video evidence. Danny took his shoes off and put them on top of the partition.

He and Jack must have been fist-fighting because Danny's watch was found on the floor. Rounds were sprayed all over the place. Danny wasn't dead, yet and Jack tried to get the gun out of his hand and because there was a lot of blood, he had to do it carefully. Jack walked away when he couldn't get the gun immediately. Then he took out his 45-automatic and came around yelling as Danny was trying to pull himself up. He shot the round right in Danny's spine. Danny went down to the floor, and Jack shot him again, almost blowing his head off.

Jack went outside to the parking lot out back and saw Yuma PD. They had their guns pointed at him and said, "Get your hands up!"

As he was walking out of the building, Jack was on the phone talking to his wife, "I have to give up, if I don't, they're going to kill me!"

Jack never got the death penalty. He got life in prison because he was under the influence of methamphetamines.

Mike made it to the hospital. He knew he was dying, and he was anxious to see his pregnant wife. He died later during surgery.[95, 96, 97, 98]

I thought, *That was a horrible death! Mike was my neighbor, and his wife is pregnant and ready to have a baby.* I believe Danny Elkin's murder was an unfortunate incident, hopefully not connected to this case, but I could never prove it. Danny was a trusted friend.

Chapter 27: Larry Encouraged to Back Down; Yuma, AZ

1996

Jeff and Randy called Larry a couple of months later and said, "Larry, we've got this informant, he's able to buy some drugs for you right now, come meet us."

"Okay, I'm on my way."

They were going to meet me at the Chilton Hotel, where I loved French fries and iced tea. This was my favorite place to meet them.

After waiting thirty minutes and I hadn't shown, they called me, "Larry, what's going on?"

"They sent me over to the airport. I have to pick something up. I should be there in about 15 minutes."

Eventually, I made it. This happened often. Sometimes I couldn't meet them at all because they would send me off to do things that just took too long. It became difficult for the private investigators to connect with me when they had information, or a buy set up. I had to watch out for my job, and I couldn't be too defiant.

I put in a lot of hours after work to deal with the private investigators because they were in town, 24/7 churning out new information.

<><><>

Jeff dominated the Yuma area, and because of him, the car rental girls would call to let him know when certain people came to town. The girls would call with all the information: where the person was going to be staying, a phone number, etc. Also, there were only two or three airlines that came into Yuma at that time. Some of the girls with the airline would call Jeff and say, "So-and-so just arrived. He's on the manifest list." Or "This guy's going to LA."

When Jeff knew someone was going to Los Angeles, he would call Randy and let him know. Randy would go to LAX or wherever the target was flying into and try to follow them from there. That was in the days when you didn't have to have a ticket to get past security. Randy would just walk up to the gate. That cramps their style today.

<><><>

In early summer of 1996, United States Attorney Janet Napolitano and her aide came to see me at the Yuma Office and talked about the Meraz investigation. Larry showed them photos of the two miniature white houses and talked about the tunnel between the Meraz homes.

The aide said, "Oh, I've been there."

I was shocked and said, "You're telling me you've been to the Meraz house?"

A person doesn't go in that house without seeing Olegario doing dope.

He responded, "Yeah!"

I zoomed into the guy, and I wanted to know why he went there.

When Ms. Napolitano saw this interaction between her aide and me, she walked away from us to the other side of the room. I asked the aide again, "Why did you go into that house?"

He said, "Well, it was part of the work I did with Senator Ed Pastor. I went there for some conference connected to produce production."

The aide knew he had done something wrong because my attention was now focused on him. I started to focus on the aide with Senator Pastor going to the Meraz house. The aide ended the conversation with me.

Janet walked away from her aide and me and didn't mention the Meraz case again. I knew that the Meraz investigation was closed for good. However, the aide met with Olegario inside his home in Mexico. It proves the Meraz brothers were right to tell Pedro and Enano DEA would never arrest them.

By the end of year five, AUSA Richard Dreamer sent me a letter saying you've got to stop this and bring the Meraz investigation to an end.

The first year of the investigation, with the help of the private investigators, I was sending fantastic information back to DEA Legal Department in Washington D.C about the Meraz involvement in the attempted murder of Don Ware and Roy Stevenson. In 1996, DEA Legal Department in Washington sent me a letter stating this is the best case ever on the Meraz, keep up the good work. The legal department said, "You have enough to prosecute the brothers."

This was unbelievable that I had enough to prosecute the Meraz brothers for the attempted murders[99] and their drug activities in the United States. My boss stated, "You have them indicted."

I felt like I had the proof for AUSA Dreamer in Phoenix to present the evidence to the Federal Grand Jury in Arizona. I had the Meraz brothers on audio recordings and drug evidence purchase with the help of Pedro and Enano!

<>>

When the private investigators came on board in 1991, I had several sources. I had a close relationship with Pedro and Enano, especially Pedro. I was already well into the case, and Randy and Jeff were giving me so much information that kept me getting deeper into the situation. I got emotionally involved in it. I was told directly to stop the investigation, but it was too late. I knew there was some corruption, but just not how much. I lost all trust with the cops when I left for Colombia.

The private investigators still had two more years of investigation. This happened because the government couldn't tell the private investigators to stop. This was the perfect private-public partnership. From my perspective, if sources like the private investigators were going to keep providing information, I felt an obligation to do keep doing my part. At least meet with them if there's something that leads to buying drugs, it's criminal not to proceed.

I kept pushing, even though I was being told by my boss and the AUSA office not to. But at some point, how does the law enforcement supervisor say to an agent to back off? How do you do that without explaining the reason? My supervisor may not have known the truth; he was just told from his higher-ups that I had to back off this thing.

At some point, since they couldn't really tell me to back off without having to explain to me national security issues, it wouldn't be legitimate national security issues. So then, they just tried to divert me by transferring me from Yuma.

There were lots of people at the AUSA office doing things covertly and overtly. The end for this case occurred one day at the AUSA Attorney's office during a discussion. I was upset about not getting help in Yuma, and one of the attorneys took the file and said, "The AUSA office can't do anything else," and slid it over to the other attorney.

I was thinking: What does that mean, they can't do anything?

At this point, I was instructed by AUSA Jimmie Lost in a roundabout way to put the case to rest. AUSA Richard Dreamer was no longer working the case. Dreamer was removed from the case for unknown reasons. I had several meetings with the United States Attorney's office, and after a while, they took a portion of the case file and shoved it over to the guy I didn't know.

Chapter 28: Larry Becomes Discouraged; Yuma, AZ

1996, Larry

Jerry Pearce tried to make me look like I walked on water. He told me, "You're DEA. You're a federal agent. You've got all the access!" Turning to the waitress, he said, "Get the boy some French fries and iced tea, here."

The government doesn't see it that way. Jeff was getting too close, and I started hearing his name in statements like, "Jeff better watch his back!" They were coming in full force for Jeff, and they were going to have him.

The AUSAs in Phoenix had everything I provided them. I knew in my heart that I had the Meraz's. Especially when an attorney from the Department of Justice in Washington DC Chief Counsel told me, "You've got it."

They sent everything back to me, showing all the charges and who should be indicted. I knew something was wrong when I was at the AUSA office, and they didn't want to do anything. The next thing I knew, I was still the case agent in charge, but the case was coming to an end. It was a slow death.

<><><>

Mark Spencer was going to help me make the big purchase to develop credibility or possibly buy even more from the Meraz's. After Mark and his intel agent searched the Grande business in Mexico, he never mentioned the case again. Whatever happened down there, it changed the nature of the case and Marks' support.

Since 1990, I had targeted the Meraz operations and finally learned the brothers had become "untouchable" by DEA and other law enforcement agencies. I told Jeff and Randy, "Do you see what's going on here in Yuma?" The abuse and corruption in our law enforcement is in the wrong hands. Like the Meraz's niece of INS at the border. I said to Jeff, "The AUSA office in Phoenix and the local cops in Yuma have targeted you twice for illegal activities."

Jeff's name was on that federal indictment created from the AUSA office. I said, "Jeff, I made it go away by telling the AUSA office and the cops in Yuma that you were helping me by providing information on law enforcement corruption and Meraz criminal activities. The AUSA and the cops didn't want to stop harassing you." I would be leaving Yuma soon.

Most United States Attorney's would die to have a case with a federal agent making a hand-to-hand buy. I had all the pieces of evidence for the AUSA. Pedro had everything on the conspiracy and about the Meraz brothers trying to kill the two DEA agents, and the phone calls going back and forth from the brothers.

The AUSA Phoenix office had all this factual evidence and details against the Meraz brothers, and they're not going to arrest anyone?

Pedro told me, "I went five years to federal prison, and all I did was make a phone call to a guy to introduce an undercover DEA agent. I didn't even know he was an agent. He wanted me to help him buy some coke. I plead guilty to conspiracy for making a phone call to a dope dealer."

I told Pedro and Enano, "My hands are tied. Everything I have is discovery, and it will be released through the judicial process later to José Jonas. The Meraz brothers and Blue Finn Seafood Company will see everything that happened in this Meraz investigation."

The Meraz's and the Blue Finn Seafood Company weren't going to leave me alone. They were after me! Someone even found my car. One morning when I went to go to the office, I had a flat. Someone had put a spike to one of the tires on my personal car. I found guts in a plastic bag in my backyard. Another morning my windshield was broken out, and the perpetrator left the photo of me taken by the Commandanté.

Yuma P.D. set up temporary surveillance on my residence.

Castillo told me, "It's time to go. Enough is enough! I want you out of here! Get out of here, get out of Yuma, get out of Arizona. Get a transfer; do something."

He wrote to headquarters that things were getting worse and I had a leak. He also wrote to them that there was a lot of corruption involved, and I had threats made to me. Everyone was running away from this case. I'm sure the CIA was all over this thing. Without a doubt!

The case started disappearing, slowly without my even realizing it. Mark was never involved with me and the case again.

<><><>

Later, as the case was disappearing, Mr. Bonner said to me, "Larry, where would you like to go?"

"I'd like to go to Madrid, Spain."

"Okay, let me see what I can do. You know Larry, I never knew what the agents were dealing with." He said, "I was always isolated from the problems you agents had." He was only meeting the people in high management.

There was a lot of information that Jeff, Randy, Erik, and John had given me, but what started to shut this case down was the Blue Finn Seafood Company. CIA began to get involved with an agent at the United States Customs working at the company. The agent was a brilliant narcotics cop. I made it very clear to the agent that the private investigators had given me the name of Mario Camaron. I knew these private investigators were good at what they did. I didn't provide information to them, but things leaked out because of my office, and they didn't want the investigators around. The longer I kept going, and these private investigators kept shaking the tree, so all the fruit and corruption from law enforcement was falling, it was getting out of control – too many leaks.

Dianne DeMille PhD, Larry Hardin, Jeffrey Pearce, Randy Torgerson

Chapter 29: Jeff and FBI; Fresno, CA

1997, Jeff

Larry told me, "You survived, but you paid the price. Jerry was sitting back and letting you take chances as long as he was getting the results he wanted. I had to stop you because Jerry called and asked me to slow you down. You know why? Because you were getting too close. You were flirting with about every girl in town and getting information that law enforcement couldn't get."[100]

Once the case was over, the FBI had a search warrant for my home and Jerry's office.

I got the call from two FBI agents from Phoenix. They asked me about Yuma, the Meraz's, and everything else.

I thought, Maybe they're going to do something about it now.

Then they switched gears and started asking about my uncle and campaign contributions. I told them I knew about Uncle Jerry giving $50 to one of the guys running for sheriff. Then, they asked about the chief of police in San Luis, AZ, Jack Pollard, and his successor.

"Why are you asking me about guys who are law enforcement? Why don't you fricken' focus on the Meraz organization and convict the criminals? Go after the bad guys."

Then they asked, "And, what was your relationship with Larry Hardin?"

"Larry and I worked together. Our relationship was professional. He was always professional. Did we have a beer together? Yeah! There's no crime there. And any information that was provided was provided one way. And that was his way. We provided to him. Michael Hope said we could share information, but it had to be information I offered him.

They said, "We're going to fly out, and we'd like to sit down and talk to you about all this stuff."

I thought this was about the case and called Jerry, "Heads up! This is the deal," and I went on to tell him what they asked me and that they'd be coming over to talk.

Jerry responded, "Well, I don't know what this could be about."

He's always that way — very low key.

Two FBI agents came to the house the next evening, and we sat down at my kitchen table. I had the strangest feeling, so I had my buddy come over. I wanted a witness. The agents sat on one side, and my buddy and I sat on the other.

The agents questioned me about receiving government documents. The FBI governs these documents. They were what every police department accesses when they pull someone over. I knew this because I was technically a cop. Sworn in by San Luis PD, and also the Cocopah Tribal Police. I knew that having these documents didn't matter, because either one of these PDs could have given them to me. You can't just purchase them.

One of the guys was on me, "Were you flirting with the dispatcher down there?"

"Yeah."

"And you were flirting with the clerk?"

"Yeah."

He missed one, so I told him, "And that other one, too."

"Oh, we didn't know about that one. I guess we should let your wife know what you're doing here."

"Well, you can put it in your notes. I don't care what you tell my wife!"

"Are you proud of that?"

"Kinda!"

"Oh, you're some kind of a smart ass, dude!"

"You're asking about a list. I spent five years of my life trying to put criminals in jail. I'm providing you guys with information, and this is where you're going? If you're still looking into the Meraz's, let me know and I'll tell you what I know. Are you guys off your rockers?"

"We have nothing else to say to you, Mr. Pearce."

As they left, I was thinking: Ah, shit. This isn't over! Not by a long shot!

At 6:45 a.m. the next day, I heard someone banging loudly at my front door.

When I opened the door, these same two agents walked in flashing their badges, saying, "FBI search warrant." It looked like the entire office of the FBI in Fresno were there with cars up and down my block. You'd think I was Al Capone!

They cuffed me, sat me down on the couch, and cuffed my wife. She had kidney failure and was late to a dialysis appointment. They wouldn't let her leave, so I jumped up off the couch and said, "Listen here, you motherfuckers! You will let her go because if something happens to her, we'll be so wealthy, I won't have to worry about a thing!"

The agent in charge said, "Let her go!" They un-cuffed her and sent her on her way.

Then they un-cuffed me and went through everything. I had some stuff like a fake Arizona license plate that I used on my vehicle when I came into town. I would take off my CA plate and put on the AZ plate. They told me, "You can't have this!"

"Okay."

They found the two IDs I had and said, "You can't have these!"

"Why not?"

"You didn't go through ALEA…"

"Look at the back." On the back, it said, "San Luis Police Department, Jack Pollard, term: indefinite."

They collected it all with some government information I had in an old briefcase and all my ATM receipts. I had tons of ATM receipts. I don't know why I kept them over the years.

I asked them, "What are you going to do with my ATM receipts?"

"Well, this is to show you were in Yuma."

"I know I was in Yuma. I'm not denying that."

Were they looking for the red book from Blue Finn Seafood Company?

There were ten federal agents at my house searching the whole house, my backyard, and the attic. I'm not sure what they were looking for. They hit Jerry's office at the same time with seven more agents. They don't even have that many federal agents in the entire Fresno office. This was a big deal!

My parents showed up and sat with me. The agents took everything they found, and when they left, they wanted to shake my hand. I told them, "Get the hell out of here!"

Two weeks later, I got a letter from the United States Attorney's office in Phoenix that said I was now the target of a federal investigation. The claim was theft of government property.

I was working from home at the time, as a licensed P.I. I took a box and stuffed it with the link analysis that I made, the red telephone book from Blue Finn Seafood Company, along with a few other things, and walked over to my next-door neighbor's house. I told him to put them in the attic, and I'd get it later.

I went to see a friend of mine who was a criminal lawyer. I told him what happened, and he called to find out who was handling this case. I heard him say it was Jimmy Lost.

"Jimmie Lost!" My mouth dropped! He was the AUSA who took the case and made it go away. I had already told him about my altercation with James in Yuma.

So, when my attorney friend had him on the phone, he said, "Yeah, Lost, do you know who you're prosecuting? You know the guy you went and had drinks with that night and got drunk? He was working on the Meraz family?"

Lost said, "I think this is much ado about nothing. I'm not going to file the case."

194

Then just as suddenly as it started, it went away!

I was thinking there were some scary moments. When you get a letter that saying you're a target of a federal investigation, it's an uncomfortable feeling. Especially when you're trying to do a good deed, it just didn't feel right.

At that time, Larry was in Bogota, Colombia and when he heard I got hit, he said, "Man! What's going on here?"

Later Larry commented, "Jeff handled that search warrant well, but what the FBI did was wrong."

I took it personally. I mean, it was really personal! And at one point, I sat there and said to myself, *Man they really came at me! And, that's not the end of it.* I even lost my job because of it.

From my standpoint, there's no love lost. I didn't speak to my uncle anymore. On the last day when he fired me, the case was over, and he just walked in and said, "I don't have a place for you in my firm anymore."

There was no, "Thank you for everything you've done for me; all the money you made me, and your allegiance to me."

There was no loyalty. He also fired his own son.

Jerry passed away a few months ago. I was hoping he would read this on his deathbed and get an epiphany that what he did was wrong. He and my father, his brother, did not talk to each other for 25 years. That was because my dad was the executor of my grandmother's estate. He wouldn't talk to my father. It was ridiculous!

We must credit some of our business today to this case, our drive, etc. Jerry was generous to a fault. He gave us bonuses every year. We had to generate information, or we were useless.

It's not like working for the government where you get paid every month. Uncle Jerry was about getting us into as much debt as he could. He would say, "We're all going rollerblading, riding bikes, shooting bows and arrows." We would each buy our own equipment. He didn't care how we got it, but we would all do it. I couldn't afford shit at the time. But he was a master manipulator!

195

He knew how to push my buttons. I was always looking for his approval.

He was my mentor. I looked up to him. When he said I did a good job, that set my juices going for a good, long time. He held that kind of shit hostage.

This was my uncle, my flesh and blood. He would sit there and literally encourage me to have sex with women so I could get information, knowing full well I was married and had a kid. He would encourage me and talked me into it. And then, on top of it, if I was meeting with somebody and he was there, he would take photos of me with them. This is the kind of prick I was working with.

Randy told me, "I don't think that was it, with Jerry. You would stand up to him more than anybody, and he didn't like that. That was the real crux of why you had to leave."

Larry commented to me, "This was personal for Jerry. I think he relied on you too much. He rode you hard about everything."

Randy added, "We looked up to him. He gave everyone a ration of shit. He would give John and I almost the same amount of shit, 'Why aren't you producing as much as Jeff?' He knew how to drive us. We got a little wiser toward the end of the case, and we would mess with him."

"One time Jeff, John, and I were sitting in a hotel room, and he started asking me questions. I told him, 'We don't know where Jeff is.' And he was sitting right next to us!"

Chapter 30: Larry Transfers; Bogota, Colombia

1997

From 1990 through 1996, I was Acting Resident Agent in charge of Yuma and became a temporary GS-14 Supervisor. In the summer of 1996, after fighting with the United States Attorney's Office in Phoenix and my support of the Pearce Corporation, I quickly lost my supervisor status. There would be no more promotions for me. Three junior agents with less time on the job received their GS-14 promotion, jumping past me. My supervisor asked me to end the Meraz investigation and transfer to the Phoenix office.

I declined the transfer.

I later received a phone call from DEA Headquarters offering me three positions to transfer out of Yuma: Instructor for Domestic Training, Instructor for International Training, both at Quantico, VA., or special agent in Bogota, Colombia. Leonardo Castillo encouraged me, "If you go to Bogota, you could get your supervisor position back when you return to the states. But you've got to keep your mouth shut because it's very political at the embassy there. You're going to see things, and you just can't get involved in them. Go down there, stay out of trouble, and just do your job. Don't get involved with the politics."

All I could think was, But you can't do your job without the politics getting involved with you.

They were transferring me to Bogota to jump-start my new career. I believed I might have another chance if I took the advice of my supervisor. I decided to take the job in Bogota.

When I came back from language school to Yuma, it was unfortunate to see where the case was. It was shut down quickly by the Phoenix AUSA office.

Ms. Janet Napolitano came to Yuma with her aide right before I was leaving Yuma for language school. She looked me in the eyes and asked, "How can we resolve this case?"

I could see it in her eyes. I could see the politics, and I was thinking to myself: *This, is incredible. She wants to help now!*

DEA wanted this case to go away because they spent a lot of money, and it took a lot of effort. DEA had two agents, Don and Roy, who were almost killed by the Meraz brothers. The brothers even bragged about it!

After I left Yuma for good, agents from my old office only arrested one person, José Jonas Rodriquez, for the sample buy. José only served a short period of time, and when he was released, all the evidence I had become discovery and went into the hands of the Meraz's and everyone else in the political world.

After finishing six months of Spanish language training in Arlington, VA, in the summer of 1997, I arrived in Bogota. I immediately observed corruption and lying among agents and supervisors at the Embassy and struggled to stay away from it. I didn't say anything about what I saw.

Later, in 1998, I heard from my brother Joseph in Kentucky, that Senator Mitch McConnell and his wife Elaine Chao would be traveling to Bogota to meet with the American Ambassador and Colombia government officials about several millions of United States dollars being provided to the Colombians to fight the "war on drugs." Joseph told me he could set up a meeting for me to meet with Senator McConnell when they arrived.

Several days later, my DEA boss asked me about the connection with Senator McConnell. He told me the Senator wanted to meet with me when he arrived, but that it might not happen. I had already established myself at the American Embassy as someone who couldn't lie but would tell the truth that the "war on drugs" was lost in Bogota.

However, Joseph called me to say that the meeting with Senator McConnell was on and the meeting would be set away from the Embassy. My boss told me that I would be meeting with the Senator at a local restaurant for lunch.

Senator Mitch McConnell, wife
Elaine Chao, Catalina Hardin-
wife, & Larry R Hardin
1998 in Bogota, Colombia

My wife and I arrived early at the restaurant, and within a few minutes, Senator McConnell and his wife entered, followed by the Ambassador and DEA supervisors. Senator and Mrs. Chao personally greeted us. The Senator and I talked about life in Colombia as we entered a large dining area. At the enormous dining table, one of the staff members from the Embassy told my wife and me to sit at the end of the table.

I was about to sit down when the Senator asked me to sit across the table from him. Mrs. Chao moved to the end of the table to my chair, next to my wife. I looked at my DEA Supervisors, and the Ambassadors faces as the seating arrangements were adjusted. I knew I would need to be careful with my words at the dining table.

The Senator asked me about my dad and brother. He had kind words about them and talked about how Joseph helped him win the election in Kentucky. As the Senator continued to talk about my family, I quickly glanced towards my wife at the end of the table. My wife and Mrs. Chao were laughing and not paying any attention to what was going on at the other end of the table.

The Senator looked directly into my eyes. I was thinking: *Oh, no, here comes the political question from the Senator.*

He asked me what I thought about the drug trafficking problems and the money that would be given to Colombia to fight the war on drugs.

Wow! I immediately looked in the Senator's eyes without thinking politically and said, "The Colombians don't care about our culture or our way of life. They only care about our money and what they can take from us."

Everyone at the table became quiet. I knew I failed to answer the question correctly. I was in trouble. But I believed in telling the truth about why the Colombians should not get our hard-earned tax dollars just to waste it.

The Senator smiled at my bold statement of truth, without any political bullshit. I nervously smiled back at the Senator, and suddenly, the DEA supervisors interrupted to tell the Senator of all the wonderful results they had from dismantling the cocaine labs.

The Ambassador followed by mentioning the excellent working relationships with the Colombian government. Senator McConnell continued to smile and looked at me while the Ambassador and DEA people talked about the great job they were doing in Colombia.

I was thankful the Senator didn't ask me any more questions about the war on drugs. I never said another word at lunch.

While the Ambassador and DEA supervisors continued their political bullshit about why they needed the money, the Senator and I looked down to the other end of the table. My wife and Mrs. Chao were still laughing. They were unaware that I just ended my chances of ever being promoted to a DEA supervisor. They were oblivious to what had just happened between the Senator and me.

When lunch was finished, the Senator and I walked outside together with our wives. Senator McConnell asked me to stay in touch. I said, "I'll never forget this meeting."

The Senator and his wife were a nice couple, and my wife received a Christmas card and a photo of us at the luncheon from Mrs. Chao.

Today, Senator McConnell is the majority leader of the Republican Senate, and Mrs. Elaine Chao is the U.S. Department of Transportation Secretary under President Trump.

<><><>

While in Colombia, I was a duty agent for all calls from the United States and any other activities outside the United States as of November 1998. It was the worst assignment with regards to sexual assault. It was Sodom and Gomorrah, indeed an evil place to work. The Colombia women were beautiful, sweet, aggressive, and eager to have sex with Americans, especially anyone working at the Bogota American Embassy. Many married DEA agents fell into the trap of open sex, and some divorced their wives to marry younger Colombian girls. My wife worked at the Embassy as a Counselor Officer and kept a close watch over me.

Thank God, my wife was my angel who protected me from the evil one. The devil really worked on me with a lot of temptation in Colombia.

When I left Yuma, my supervisor told me if I could work well in my new position, I'd get my promotion.

But I couldn't keep my mouth shut because that's who I am. When I saw someone doing something wrong, I spoke my mind and told them. I really resisted when the private investigators started telling me about Norman being corrupt and how the information was leaking out from the DEA office.

After several months in Colombia, I got a phone call from the Chief Legal Counsel office at DEA headquarters in D.C. The attorney wondered how things went with the Meraz case, "What happened? We did the work for you. All you had to do was take the packet to an attorney."

"It's not going to happen, and I'm still not sure why. If you can do something to get it through, that would be great." I never heard from him again.

About two months later, I was awakened from a sound sleep. It was about 2:00 a.m. when the phone rang. I was trying to wake up and picked up the receiver and just said, "Yes."

The voice said, "Agent Frank Moreno was killed in a fuego [fire]."

Frank was working at the Bogota American Embassy. He was a good friend of mine with DEA. The day Frank was murdered, he was out with some friends at a night club from the Mexican Embassy.

I said immediately, "Who is this?" It was a marine at the American Embassy. I told him, "What? Is this a joke?"

The voice repeated, "Frank Moreno was killed."

I hung up the phone and called my boss to explain the call.

My boss said, "Son-of-a-bitch! Larry, call me back."

I called Stacy, Frank's wife. When I called, she said, "I don't know where Frank is! He's not answering his phone or his pager. I'm worried about him."

I didn't want to alarm her and thought it would be better to talk with her in person. I just told her, "When Frank gets home, have him give me a call. I need some help from him."

I called back my boss about the conversation with Stacy. Now, my wife was sitting up in bed.

The boss told me, "You need to get to the hospital. You're going to meet the Embassy nurse. When you get there, go with the nurse. Frank's been shot."

I immediately jumped out of bed. My wife was following me, grabbing her clothes.

I told her, "Stay home."

She said, "No, Stacy needs my help."

A 9mm bullet killed agent Frank. That same bullet entered his chest cutting his aorta and exited his back, hitting a young Colombian boy in the side of his neck. Frank died quickly. The boy passed away the next day.

Late that night, I watched four people examine Frank's body. They moved him from side to side on the table, locating the gunshot wound, taking photos. His body lay there naked on the table while they moved him around.

As I watched, I was thinking: *Here, lies my buddy who would steal my apple from my desk and always told me what was going on in the office.* Frank always had my back in the office and out in the field doing operations when we were in California.

They moved Frank's body to another location for the autopsy. The examiner, wearing a large leather apron, rubber

202

gloves and rubber boots up to his knees, asked with my wife standing next to me, "Do you want to observe while I examine Frank?"

I said, "No." That was Frank's body, and I didn't want to watch when they cut him up.

After a few hours, they brought his body out for me to examine.

My wife had no words as she looked at the tag wrapped around Frank's right big toe.

They put a white cooler next to his body. I learned later that the cooler contained his brain and organs. Frank's body was a mess from his body fluids when they opened his chest. I told them, "Can you clean him up now? Comb his hair." They did. I will always remember that white cooler.

That night, one bullet killed two people. I helped take care of Frank's body for three days until Frank went home wrapped in an American flag over his coffin.

Soon after, an agent told me that Frank's death was a bump in the road. They needed to move on. I suddenly felt like this was one big lie with the war on drugs. I cried inside for Frank's death. I felt his life meant nothing to the DEA agents in Bogota.

Dianne DeMille PhD, Larry Hardin, Jeffrey Pearce, Randy Torgerson

Epilogue

Larry

After a short three years (1997-2000) in Colombia, I went to back to San Diego. I retired from the DEA in July 2011. Now I share my experiences teaching criminal justice to students coming into law enforcement at local universities and colleges. I also own a private investigation business and on occasion, volunteer to visit military veterans, law enforcement agents, and officers in hospice.

I had a great job with DEA. I enjoyed it. I believe I was in that job and went to Yuma for a reason: to target the brothers for what they did to Don and Roy. At the same time, I realize it was a dangerous atmosphere. I felt guilty about not getting to prosecute the Meraz brothers for trying to kill Don and Roy. I had an opportunity to investigate what the Meraz's were doing, and I felt I could do something about it. I was determined. I kept to myself, and that's what helped to build my character.

I believe there are only disappointments for the victims. DEA gave me a good career. I'm in good health, and I have an enjoyable retirement with a great pension. I won the lottery. Thank God.

Randy and Jeff talked to me about law enforcement skeletons in the closet. I didn't want to hear about it. I didn't want to know because I had to work with these agents and cops. I had to trust them with my life. It's part of me and who I am. I knew I had to be very cautious about how I dealt with things. It was like in Vietnam when some of the officers took a bullet in the back from fellow officers. They never made it back because one of their own men shot them.

I never got promoted. I wanted to become an Assistant Special Agent in Charge (ASAC) which was as far as I could go in the agency. I had the personality and the integrity. However, I never got the connections with the right people with the same integrity. Some of the guys I worked with were more concerned about their careers. Some agents stayed away from my private investigators because these guys were shaking the trees, and the fruit was beginning to fall. Some of the guys in law enforcement were fearful of falling fruit.

The agents who played the game got promoted. It broke my spirit when I had to let the case go and head to Colombia. I knew too much about the Meraz brothers' dope activities and the corruption in Yuma. I was given a second chance.

I lost some good friends because of the work I was doing. And I lost the case because someone else in law enforcement leaked information to the Meraz's. I could never cross the line I was very loyal and believed I had mutual respect for every agent in the DEA organization. They were my family! I was so disappointed with myself for failing to honor Don and Roy.

I was confused about what I should do next with my career. I learned that corruption was deeper in law enforcement than I ever imagined. Too many agents were thinking about their futures and ignoring what was right. I tried to reveal the truth. I knew the information I had was spot on. My sources and the private investigators opened the door for me to develop the evidence needed to indict the Meraz brothers and the corrupt cops who worked for them.

It became more apparent that DEA, AUSA, and other official organizations didn't want the case solved. It's almost like they wanted me to fail. My first supervisor didn't even say goodbye to me when he left Yuma. I was really frustrated. For many agents, all they wanted was their promotion while I was trying to do what was right.

Look at the AUSA's Michael Hope. He later went on to the CIA. We had hit it off, and he encouraged me to go after these guys. But then DEA, FBI, and the AUSAs were all freaked out that I was getting too close to know everything involved. This had never happened before with other agents, and it made me a danger to DEA.

I thought about what AUSA Richard Dreamer said, "You can't have Pedro and Enano testify because they're doing drugs with the Meraz's. I can't prosecute this case." When I took my CIs to meet with AUSA Dreamer, he was very disrespectful to them. When I stood up to walk them out, he told me, "You can't do that as a DEA agent." But I did, and that was the moment I realized I wasn't going to see this case through.

I remember thinking: What are you talking about? You need my CIs. They're going to testify that they got close with the Meraz brothers.

If the private investigators hadn't been involved, I probably never would have gotten so close to prosecuting. But it also wouldn't have been as stressful, because while I was working some significant cases, I was also working this one behind the scenes. When the P.I.s got involved, they pushed me, and they pushed the DEA. I needed them. Blue Finn Seafood Company was too much for me to handle alone.

DEA defined me, not only as a person but spiritually. I struggle with determining the truth about life. "Live your life, now." Looking back, I think it's about knowing the truth, and we should enjoy every moment in life. I don't feel bitterness with what happened with the DEA or my cases. Some cases were easy to adjudicate, and some were difficult because of greed on both sides of the fence. It's amazing what money can do to people in the world of drugs and narcotics.

It's incredible what I learned about working narcotics for almost 24 years. I had to stay focused and just try to do what I knew was right in my heart. I decided not to follow to the dark side, or as they say, the Camino del Diablo, the Path of the Devil. That was my struggle working narcotics.

I was meant to represent what is right, and yet I saw so much evil in my job. This was more of a challenge because I knew what was right, I knew the purpose of my career, yet the evil I was going after was a powerful thing. The criminals knew what they were doing. They knew it was wrong and immoral, but they tried to justify all of it to themselves.

I was disappointed, not so much with the Meraz's. They were just a family operating a business. They were giving the American people what they wanted: the dope. It was just a business for them, albeit a very violent business. People got hurt and killed. It was the same in Mexico and Colombia. It was part of their job. Like me, going to work with narcotics, the criminals were out there pushing dope across the border into the United States.

Working at the border, I didn't see a majority of white people coming across, but I wasn't targeting Mexicans. I was targeting narcotics traffickers – anyone involved with illegal crime against the U.S.

The most dangerous thing I encountered was the temptation of lust, money, and sex. In a situation where money was found, no one could claim it. I made it through with the blessing of my faith, and for that, I worked hard. In a world like this, I was doing my job. I did put people in jail, but most of them were very poor and just trying to make a living.

The triumph for me was keeping my faith. Not with my wife or my family, but with my confidence. I stayed focused on that. That was my biggest challenge.

I saw a few people I knew personally killed on the job. Like Richie Fass and Frank Moreno. Danny Elkins and Michael Crowe. All hard workers and good people. Danny wanted to work on the Meraz case with me. I blame those who didn't want to prosecute the case.

I had to wait five years before doing anything with the information I learned on this case.

Under the law, I could move on with new information the private investigators kept feeding me. I could have kept going if I wanted to. If there was a conflict between what I could do and what my supervisors told me I shouldn't do, I would go ahead anyway.

The burr in the saddle of this whole case was they couldn't control the private investigators. DEA and other agencies couldn't tell the PIs to stop. They could monitor me by not allowing me to go on, but the PIs didn't work for them.

The private investigators I worked with were innocent. They still had the naïve dream, the American ideal. They were "go-getters" and knew how to get the information. Jeff was very young and emotional and took it personally. He had just come out of the military and didn't have the law enforcement background. This type of work was different than the military. He began to lose his way.

The PIs were young, and this was a big case. Jeff explains that they knew what they were doing, but they weren't aware of all the ins-and-outs and the little tricks they learned along the way. They were learning new things on the job, all the time. The hard part was learning that criminals are masquerading as good guys. None of them knew how to deal with that.

No matter how good the people I found, the PIs weren't cops or agents, and I knew I could trust them. But I had to be very careful not to provide them with any DOJ/DEA documents. That's why the FBI searched Jeff. They ultimately wanted to come after me. FBI knew I was shaking the bushes real hard for corruption. The FBI questioned Randy about certain documents as well as the NCIC reports he obtained when he was trying to put undercover drug deals together in the Los Angeles area with the Los Angeles Sheriff's office.

<>⟨⟩<>
Jeff

I honed my interview and interrogation skills. I learned how to work cases and homicide. Jerry taught me a lot. It was quite the experience! I kept myself abreast of the law and how it applied to investigators. 1 told Jerry, "I'm going to run the company one of these days!"

I was intrigued. Initially, this was a case having to do with stocks and Bill Grover. When we got into it, we found we were involved with a drug case. I didn't have the experience of dealing with drugs and some of the other things that came along with this case. But I was confident in myself. My wife and I had a young daughter and lived a decent lifestyle. My uncle paid me well.

As I got more involved with this case, it became a mission for me. The more information I could find, the harder my uncle was on me. He really wanted the information. If we couldn't provide or develop the information, then we weren't much good to him. It caused me to think more outside of the box. He would say that to me all the time!

"Any normal detective will do what they were taught at the academy, but what they can't be taught is to think outside of the box."

I asked him, "What does that mean? Think outside of the box?"

"Be creative in what you do, understand that there's more information out there that you haven't touched yet. Don't take what you initially get as the truth. Always assume there's more."

He told me there are many ways to cross-reference and confirm what people are saying. I didn't know what that meant at first. But, I was honing my skills all the time, and I had a knack for getting people to confess to me. I learned what he meant by cross-referencing what was said.

I have a good memory, and still have today, that's better than most people. When I'm interviewing someone, I remember what they say. It may be an hour to two hours into the interview, and I've learned to ask questions in multiple ways to elicit the information they may be holding back.

Uncle Jerry was the master at interviewing and interrogating people. He was my teacher, but I surpassed him. I could take what Uncle Jerry taught me and sharpen it to a point where I became an expert at interrogation and investigation. With my drive, I could keep pushing. I could manipulate people to get them to give me what I wanted. It has become a more pronounced ability.

This case was the one I'll never forget. It taught me a lot of life lessons. It was most traumatic for me because when I started, I was a red-white-and-blue kind of guy. I didn't believe the government was corrupt in any way. That hadn't even crossed my mind. It never occurred to me that the government was involved in the things we uncovered.

Because of my youth and naiveté, I was affected in many ways. I didn't want to believe the corruption with law enforcement. I wanted to think that the US Attorney's office was always right; the cops we dealt with were always right. They were charged with the responsibility, and I believed they would do what they were supposed to do without being corrupt. But I learned that wasn't the case.

I was in over my head a few times. A lot of times, I was doing things I thought were appropriate. But they weren't. Now, at age 49, I realize these things were not becoming of me. They caused me issues in my marriages. I know I'm only human. I was a young guy, and I made mistakes in my youth.

I let the wanton desire to get information to outweigh my moral compass. I was brought up better than that. My uncle talked me into things I shouldn't have done. But he was my mentor. Now that I look back, I realize he should've been a better guide for me. I'm disappointed in myself, and if I could do it all over again, I would change some of the things I'd done in my work.

Randy and I looked at it as just another case when we began. We had no clue about where it would go. We knew we were on the right track when Larry would say, "Be careful!"

Bringing all this up gives me an uncomfortable feeling because of all the stress that went with it. The last thing I need is to cause more deficits in my life. I don't want to cause my family any pain.

I don't want to create more problems by putting this story into the book. However, I want it told that we went to all measures to gather the information needed. And, no matter how you look at it, it still affects all three of us, as well as our families and children.

This case changed my life. Being charged criminally in a court of law was something I never imagined I'd ever face. It's never been a part of who I am or who I was.

I realize now that I was set up. I was dealing with forces much more powerful than I. It caused me great and extensive pain. I survived. I realize without those experiences; I wouldn't be as successful as I am today in my business. These experiences helped mold me into the person I am today.

My relationships and marriages over the years have helped add to those experiences. Because of the strengths, I had back then; I realize now there's no problem I can't overcome. The only thing I have to worry about is God. That's it!

I can't take back the things I did. Some things I don't want to take back. Some things I'm happy that I learned. There are a lot of things I wish I had the courage to do better. I'd like to use more common sense and be morally better than I was at that time. All of these things have come to me with age. I had to learn the hard way, and I finally did learn.

There were many triumphs. Even though the case didn't proceed the way we wanted and there were situations out of our control, like not having the say-so of the United States District Attorney and the DA in Yuma. The things I did and the things I experienced were all critical to becoming a better investigator. I was exposed to corruption in law enforcement, and I learned the Meraz family wanted to put up "Wanted" posters of me in Mexico because I was getting too close to their organization. I learned so much from the experience. Many law enforcement people have never experienced some of the things I did at such a young age. Learning something through experience is undoubtedly the best way.

212

<>< ><>

When the case concluded, I was fired. The day my uncle came in and told me he no longer had a place for me in his organization was probably one of my better days! During the case, I was fired so many times that I had a box under my desk with all my keepsakes. I knew eventually everything was going to come to a head. I took out the box, a picture of my daughter from my desk and went into Uncle Jerry's office. He was standing there, looking out the window, and I said, "Jerry."

He turned around and said, "Yep."

I went over and shook his hand and said, "I just want to thank you for everything you taught me." Then I walked out of the building.

I wasn't angry. I wasn't anything. I just thanked him. I knew it wasn't going to stop there. I was going to move forward and do my own thing.

I subsequently started my own firm. Uncle Jerry gave me the ability to do those things and make something of myself. I've been successful in my practice now for 21 years. I've done well. I've loved some women. Now, I have my daughter and my son, and I adore both, with every bit of my heart. I've realized that not everything is black and white, and I've been stringent in certain areas in my relationships. I've always thought everything should be my way. I've learned that everything is not always going to be my way.

This book has brought up a lot of emotions inside me. Every time I think about it, I remember other things that happened. It's like rewriting your life, and there are things you want to forget, but they can't be overlooked. I know this story needs to be heard and being listened to is part of the cleansing experience for me. Being able to be the person I ultimately need to be down the line, for my daughter, my son, and my grandchildren.

I'll always be who I am. I'm willing to be that tough, and rumble kind of guy and I'm not going to take shit from anybody. It's not how I was raised. I'm never going to back down from a challenge. That's not going to happen. Never has in my life, and it never will.

I've learned that not all battles need to be fought, and not all situations need to be won. I just know I'm a better man today than I was yesterday, and if anybody can see what transpired in this book and realize what everyone did to see this case prosecuted, from Larry, Randy, and everyone else involved including law enforcement and the United States Attorney. You can see we had an uphill battle, but we always did our best.

I sometimes wonder if I should thank God or curse Him for some of the things that happened. But I'd like to lean toward thanking Him.

I don't understand why I had to go through some of the things I did. I don't know why I am the way I am. I've accepted it. I realize that it's okay. Being me is okay. It's okay to wrap my head around the things that have happened in my life. No one's perfect.

My next steps, after 28 years doing what I do, is to take some time for myself and be there for my son, who I adore more than life itself. I want to provide him an experience where he can learn from Dad's mistakes and know that he can conquer anything he wants in life.

I'm tired! Tired of hearing problems, investigating assholes, throwing people in jail, I want my life to be happy and put a smile on my face.

<><><>

Randy

I learned a lot from the case. I learned I need to pay attention to detail, the minute details. We have to anticipate what the other side is going to do or say. It's not enough to say we know your Chinese guy in Amsterdam is making these duplicates. We need to go and see that. We need to document it happening, somehow.

It's one thing to know the criminals. We need to prove what they're doing or saying that makes them the criminals.

214

I didn't realize what I was learning at the time we were working the Meraz/Grove case. Even after we went through everything, I still didn't see it. After I had time to mature and think about it, I was able to look back and see what I learned.

I had a DEA agent threaten me, and it was the first time I worked with federal agents. I had reported things to the feds before, but I hadn't worked with them.

I can't stop thinking about how sad our country is now. There are so many things we do in our government that's overt. Much of it's for the greater good. But if it's so good, why did the AUSA not want to prosecute the case? If it was an issue of national security, they just had to tell us, and we'd have walked away. I never got why they didn't just tell us. It was so evident that they wanted us to let it go.

Now, I'm way ahead of the game. I know how the feds operate. They made me realize there's nobody to depend on. To do my work, I need to try to manipulate the system. I never did that with Larry. We talked straight up and didn't have to do the manipulation I've learned as part of my job.

Even now, working with Larry, we have trust with each other. I can call Larry about who to talk to when I'm working a case. He guides me to the right people to connect with for the work I'm doing. That goes both ways. Larry often calls me for what I can provide him. We trust each other and know that we're going to be okay. I learned to know who to trust, because of all the corruption we saw on that case. Larry would refer someone or tell us when to back off.

Ray Shorb is the same way. We still connect about who to connect with when we need some information, and I can trust Ray to be straight with me.

I was in law enforcement and didn't trust who I worked with. It was more about disagreements and wondering if they had my back. Working with Larry and Ray gave me back my confidence to know there are people who have my back.

The trust and loyalty I knew I had from Larry and Ray was more the exception than the rule.

For Larry, it got worse.

I did three months of surveillance in South Central Los Angeles of the activities of the Mexicans. We knew about Blue Finn Seafood Company and some things about the Asians and their involvement. I got connected with Sam Little when we found out about Blue Finn Seafood Company in California. Someone came to Grove Manufacturing and said they needed help.

Ray ran Blue Finn Seafood Company through the system at Los Angeles PD and then CIA came in. The DEA agent on the case was Sam Little. He told us he could share with us.

We worked with Grove Manufacturing, following their trucks. It was a criminal case. I kept thinking: *What's the connection that links with Blue Finn Seafood Company? How's the connection made?* I spent time in the archives, and Blue Finn Seafood Company came up in the files. Jeff may have seen a relationship with something in Yuma. The information was verbal, or it was something in a file that connected to Blue Finn Seafood Company.

How was this connected with Ray Shorb? Jerry's OCID, Jim Conrad, was getting ready to retire. He had some serious connections in Los Angeles with drugs, and he walked us across the hall to meet Ray Shorb.

Blue Finn Seafood Company information came to us from two places. One of Jeff's informants, a Grove truck driver, drove shrimp to Los Angeles and the Blue Finn Seafood Company. Simultaneously I was going through the archives, and once it was on my radar, I started checking the background of the Blue Finn Seafood Company. Ray Shorb had never heard of Blue Finn Seafood Company. Jeff gave me the name from an interview he conducted with one of the Grove/Grande drivers, who said there were drugs on it.

Blue Finn Seafood Company is still around. They're not good. Larry focused on the Meraz's, but when Oswaldo took his CI to the Blue Finn Seafood Company, things started taking a turn. We didn't want problems with the CIA, but we sensed they were protecting someone.

At this point in my work, I'm not afraid to talk to agents about a case. I don't tell them everything, and I have to be more manipulative. I need to convince them that there's something in it for them. Then they'll help me. For me to get an agent to do something, they've got to see the light at the end of their tunnel. Not my tunnel, their tunnel! I try to have most of the case put together so they can verify things for me. If they take it to their supervisor, then they'll work with me.

Larry never told anyone about what Jeff and I said about law enforcement. They would back off from us, because of Larry. We were very vocal in public about our work. If they had the credentials, we would talk to them about our case. We spoke to no less than 126 law enforcement agencies during the case

Today, I can say I have more than 25 years' experience, and most of my cases were prosecutable. They were typically financial cases, hard fraud, or stolen exotic car cases, etc...

After the first year or two at Pearce Corporation, when we had our roundtable meetings with all the investigators, we often discussed how frustrated Larry was getting. We talked about how we could make him feel better because we needed him to continue to work with us. He was the one who could stop the drugs coming through Grove Manufacturing. It hurt us to know his own people hounded him. Jerry knew that Larry was the only one working the Meraz case.

We never met Larry's CIs.

Larry would tell us that Jerry put us through hell, but we got the job done.

Jeff and I would not be as successful today if not for this case. During those years there was such a wealth of education we wouldn't have learned any other way. We learned about loyalty, trust, procedure, secrets, honesty, teamwork, and how to use them in the future.

When I decided to go into the private investigation field, I saw what Jerry was billing for this case. I saw there was no limit. It's harder to be a PI than it is to be a cop because, in the beginning, you have to have the experience. When cops start out, they have no experience. They get trained. They can only work on criminal cases. As a PI, I can work criminal and civil cases. There've been times I've had to convince some cops that we can work criminal cases.

In order to get law enforcement involved, two things must happen. Personality is a key factor, and second, they must have the same agenda for the case and in life. Larry, Jeff, and I have the same values and morals.

We weren't just collecting a paycheck. For us, it was about looking good. We had to make our clients look good. For Larry, he had to keep his bosses happy; however, the way he saw it, he didn't care what they thought. He just wanted to get the job done.

Larry worked with a lot of PIs before working this case. He always said, "When I met Jerry and his investigators, I saw hope that they could help me. I double-checked everything they told me, and the information was falling into place."

In 2004, I started working on an art fraud case. My client was from Japan. He owned many pieces of original Rembrandts, a lot of high-end artwork. I went to five different countries in 18 months to solve the case. The guy lived in NY and was married to a Japanese lady. He was an antiquities art dealer in downtown Manhattan. He bought many original works of art from two different auction houses, Christie's and Sotheby's.

There was a Chinese guy in Amsterdam who would spend months creating duplicates of just about any painting. He would put the original in storage for two years and then sell the copy.

When the case was about 90% done, my partner Yuki and I went to the FBI. The agent we spoke to thought we were full of shit. Then, he called us back and asked to meet again. This was over the course of a week. He had inquired at the FBI and learned they had been trying to get this guy twice before but failed.

The New York AUSA assigned two deputy AUSAs and three FBI agents to wrap up the case. The art dealer was charged federally and criminally for 26 years in prison. Through negotiations, when there was so much fraud, victims would agree to negotiate restitution to reduce their sentence. This guy made restitution. He came in with a check for $13 million and arranged to get his time down to 54 months.

A few months after the close of the case, the New York office of the FBI called and asked us to come back to their office. Robert Mueller, head of FBI wanted to give us an accommodation from the FBI for the work we had done on the art fraud case. We each got an award from Mueller, and our client gave us $20,000.

While celebrating our success, we talked with some of the agents.

They told us, "You know, some people give out awards and sometimes even cash awards. Mueller doesn't give us awards. We might get one from a local agency, but we don't get awards from Mueller! This is a big deal!"

Randy G Torgerson
2006, FBI Award

Ray Shorb retired in 1999 and moved to Montana. He's a close friend of mine to this day. I see Ray and his wife whenever I go back to Montana. He still teases me about how much overtime money I helped him make.

<><><>

Larry

After returning to San Diego, I got a phone call from Yuma DEA agent, "I was at a party and met this girl. Her father is Olegario Meraz. I looked it up and man, you were all over this case. What happened?"

I was thinking about what he said to me, another agent who wanted to prosecute the Meraz brothers. He wanted to finish where I left off.

I told the agent he would never be able to prosecute the case against the Meraz's.

He told me, "I'm going to come and see you."

I got another call from Yuma. It was the same DEA agent.

The agent asked again what had happened. I explained to the agent, "I laid everything out for the AUSA's Richard Dreamer and Jimmie Lost to prosecute. It's over. It's done."

I had sent a copy of the indictment to Washington, D.C., explaining why the Meraz brothers should be indicted based on everything I outlined.

I told him, "Look, I'm glad you want to look at the Meraz's, but it's not going to happen."

"I want to come to see you."

"Sure, I'll meet with you.

I didn't hear from him again, and that meeting never happened.

Less than three years after I retired, I got a call from Phoenix. It was a different DEA agent asking why the Meraz brothers weren't prosecuted. I told the agent, since I was now a private citizen and no longer working for DEA, I needed to be careful.

The agent understood and said, "Yes, but I need to ask you some questions about the case."

I asked the agent why he was reviewing my old case.

"I'm in Phoenix, and I was assigned to look at it. All these brothers and the Asian people! What happened?"

220

"These are good questions you're asking me, but you might as well let it go. I'm telling you right now, take the case and close it for good. There's no reason to review it."

"I want to come out to San Diego and see you."

"You can call me or come here anytime."

The agent said, "Okay, I'll see you soon."

And guess what? I never heard from him again, and he never came to see me.

Looking back, the entire experience was incredible – probably one of the best corruption cases I ever worked on, not only in Mexico but also in the United States. In my life, I never experienced anything like the kind of corruption involved in this case.

The Meraz's were never prosecuted, and they're still very active! I only got one mule, José. I believed in what I was doing. I felt so bad about this case, and I did Don and Roy wrong. That was just another slap in the face. My DEA career was over.

Years later, I was discussing the case with Jeff and Randy, and Jeff said, "Everybody should have been indicted!"

Randy added, "On conspiracy alone!"

Jeff came back with, "And, all of a sudden, it's just gone!"

Randy commented, "There's no question, out of all of us, including Larry, Jeff got the rawest end of the deal! Whether it was self-inflicted or not, he got the worst deal. Not only from the federal government but also the local police with what happened in Yuma. I would say that when Jeff got in trouble, we all got in trouble. We didn't like that he did, but we suffered, nonetheless. And Jerry made sure of that! If I got in trouble for some stupid thing, everybody else heard about it. That's just the way it was."

What if we did indict the Meraz's? I believe a lot of people would be killed, and the Meraz family would disappear. They'd never be seen again. They'd been the gatekeepers along the border and heavily connected in the community and law enforcement, and I believe that would all disappear. The Meraz's were well-connected within Chicago, Los Angeles, and New York and they bragged about it. It would have had a domino effect on the family. What that family did to children, young girls.

I don't think it would have changed me, but I would have felt that I'd done right by Don and Roy and others harmed by the Meraz's.

Acknowledgements

We want to acknowledge our families and friends who supported us throughout this endeavor to get the story into print. They stood by us twenty-six years ago and continue to support the work we do.

Dianne DeMille PhD, Larry Hardin, Jeffrey Pearce, Randy Torgerson

Biographies

Dianne DeMille, Ph.D.

Dianne has a Ph.D. in Education and has written several educational books. She has recently retired after more than 40 years in education. She is co-author of *It Started with A Pencil: Memoir, Leslie B. DeMille,* about her father and his career as an internationally renowned professional artist. The three men asked Dianne to write this story on their behalf.

Larry Ray Hardin

Larry Ray Hardin is a retired DEA agent after 30 years and currently teaches criminal law to law enforcement students, runs his own private investigating business, and volunteers to visit with military veterans, law enforcement agents and officers in hospice.

The Early Years

I grew up running in the Hollers and swimming in the creeks of Big Plum Creek, Taylorsville, Kentucky.

I was the oldest of eight children. I was a tall, skinny guy who talked too much and spoke with a strong southern drawl. My dad, Ray Hardin Junior, worked two jobs most of his life as a welder during the day and a farmer and sharecropper in the evening. My mom, Betty, called me Larry Ray, but when she got mad, she would yell "Lawrence Raymond, wait till I tell your dad."

Mom took care of my three brothers, four sisters, and me. She cooked several meals each day on a wood stove and later, got a gas stove. Most of my clothes were from second-hand stores or the church, but mom made sure they were always clean when we went to school or church. Dad made it my responsibility to make sure no one mistreated or beat up on my brothers or sisters at school. My family didn't have many material things but always had food on the table –beans, potatoes, gravy, cornbread, and sometimes a squirrel or rabbit. Sunday dinners were special. We had fried chicken, and Dad helped prepare.

I never forgot the time I worked chopping out the weeds on RT Jenney's tobacco field with Aunt Betty Jane. I was only eight years old, earning $5 for a day's work. After my first day, Dad took me to a discount clothing store and told me to pick out a pair of blue jeans and a shirt. When we got to the cashier, Dad told me to pay for my clothes. I thought he was joking. I'd been thinking about all the Big Red soft drinks and salted peanuts I was going to buy with my $5. But I paid for the clothes instead and never forgot the value of money from that experience.

Later, we lived in old Harry McKinley's three-room house next to a creek with an outhouse and a sulfurous well. The water from the well stunk like rotten eggs. On a hot summer day, I had to pinch my nose to swallow the water.

I was seven years old when Dad put a shotgun in my hands and taught me how to use it. I was shooting at empty cans and bottles. I learned that guns helped put food on the table, could help you stay out of trouble, and kept you from getting hurt.

Later, when I was 12 years old, my parents gave me a 20-gauge shotgun for Christmas. I spent many days walking in the woods behind the house with my gun, looking for squirrels and rabbits for supper. As I got older, I often thought about getting into law enforcement and protecting people.

We all lived in old Harry's three-room house for several years. Mr. Harry finally added another room, so us boys could have a bedroom of our own. The outhouse remained the same; we all had to share the "pee pot" or "outhouse." During the summer, everyone used the creek next to the house for bathing.

My grandparents lived on a farm near Mr. Harry's old house. I visited them often, helping out on the farm and taking Grandpa to the doctor or the stockyards to sell his pigs. I'll never forget the gravy, biscuits, and sausages Grandma Hardin cooked for breakfast every morning on a wood-burning stove. My brother, Jeffrey and I spent our summers helping Grandpa Hardin milk cows and push manure out of the barn twice a day. I quickly learned that cows love to shit while Grandpa Hardin pulled on their big fat udders. Sometimes Jeffrey and I would find ourselves covered with cow shit.

I helped other farmers in the area haul hay, repair fences, and cut tobacco. I also helped clean out Mr. Pop's chicken barn and Carroll Ray's hog sheds and horse stalls. At night, I spent a lot of time coon hunting with Grandpa Hardin.

I decided to quit the farm life after shoveling horse shit from a stall all day. I told Carrol Ray's son, Peanuts, "No more cleaning horse and pig shit. I'm out of here!"

<><><>

I always tried to stay out of trouble. But then I met Jimmy. He was watching my sisters, Belinda and Dee Dee playing in the all-girls church softball game at the park.

I asked him, "Hey, do you want to get naked and run across the ballpark?"

He smiled, "Yes!"

That was the only time I was ever arrested. The town cop charged me with indecent behavior. Later, the judge dropped the charge but fined me $60. Jimmy stayed in jail for two days for having some weed hidden under his car seat.

Jimmy later married Belinda.

I always wondered if she married him because she saw him naked running across the park.

<>< ><>

Later, my Uncle Larry Dale found me a job at the Texaco gas station off Interstate 245 near Louisville, Kentucky. Mr. Phillips, the manager of the Texaco station, didn't want to hire me because my hair was down to the crack of my butt, and I looked like a hippie who smoked weed. But I was able to assure him that I didn't smoke.

A few days later, I started my short career at the station – pumping gas, changing oil, and repairing tires. I wore my new green Texaco uniform with the big red star on the front of my shirt. I'll always remember Texaco's slogan, "Trust the man who wears the star."

I'll also remember all the weed and sex. Women would offer to have sex in exchange for gas, and a lot of them were married. I told Dad I would have felt guilty if I'd had sex with a married woman because I was concerned for her husband. I pledged myself, no sex with married women, only single women. Maybe it was my long hair and smile that attracted the women. Heck, I had gay men trying to pick me up for gas, but I stayed away from them.

After a few months of pumping gas, I was working alone on the night shift for the first time. Before leaving, Mr. Phillips told me, "If someone tries to rob you, don't go into the back office. Stay out in the open so others can see you, especially if law enforcement is driving by. They won't shoot you out in the open."

It was a hot summer night, and I was busy pumping gas. I put the cash in my left sock because I didn't have time to put it away in the office safe. Wearing my Texaco uniform with the star, I pumped gas and cleaned windshields for my customers.

Later that night, a gray four-door Mercury with two scruffy-looking men pulled up next to the gas pump. The driver got out of the car, went right into the front office, and looked around. The passenger jumped out and asked me to check the transmission fluid. The engine was running (because you need to keep it running while checking the fluids). I pulled up the hood and leaned over the car.

The passenger poked me in the back and whispered in my right ear, "Don't move."

I started to ask him what he was doing when he poked me again and said, "Just shut the fuck up."

Then he slapped me in the face and told me to go into the office where the driver was waiting.

I remembered what my boss told me earlier that day and told the guy, "No! There are cops everywhere."

He slapped me again and moved his hands down my legs where he found the cash. The driver and passenger both grabbed me, forcing me to go with them inside the office. I yelled at them again, "Man! Some cops might see you guys."

The driver let go of me and walked over to shut the hood of the car. He then jumped in behind the wheel. At that moment, I was in a dream-like state and thought, *They're going to shoot me in the back and leave me crawling on the ground, fighting for my life.*

The passenger let go of my arm and turned around with his small black revolver in his right hand. I was thinking: *Here's a chance to wallop this guy on the head and maybe get his gun.* But I couldn't move.

Instead, the passenger pushed the revolver into the front waist of his pants and hopped into the passenger seat. They took off and left me standing there, watching them tear down the road.

I was freaking out. I was still alive and not shot! I immediately called the police, and within minutes, they arrived at the station. I gave them a description of the robbers and their car. I said, "Two young men took the money I hid in my sock. With a gun in my back and hitting me in the face, I thought I was going to die."

The police said, "These are the same robbers who raped a woman inside her car at a shopping mall where she worked. She's lucky to be alive! So are you. They stole the woman's car and then came over here."

I'm so glad I kept the money in my sock! God knew this was not the time for me to die.

I quit my job the next day. That was the end of my gas-pumping career and wearing my green uniform with the red star.

<><><>

I joined the Navy in November of 1979 at age 25. I served six years and four months, mostly in the Marine Corps. I began as an expert rifleman and worked as a Religious Program Specialist assigned to the Chaplain's Office. In 1986, I was honorably discharged from the U.S. Navy with several Navy and Marine Corps medals and awards. I also received several degrees: an AA, BS, and two MAs, all while in the military. While stationed in Rota, Spain, I got married to a beautiful Spanish woman – a flamenco dancer and a great cook. She is my true love.

We moved back to San Diego, California. At that time, there were no cell phones, pagers, or the internet. Cities had telephone books with white page sections that listed names and businesses alphabetically, and the yellow page sections with businesses. I looked through the yellow pages for law enforcement and inquired about the Federal Bureau of Investigation (FBI) about three times. Then I saw the Drug Enforcement Administration (DEA) and didn't know what it was, so, I called them and spoke with a recruiter. He told me his story about being shot, wounded, and almost killed doing undercover work in Chicago. I thought about what he said, but it didn't deter me. It drew me closer to thinking I might want to be a DEA agent. I told him, "I have two master's degrees and just got out of the military. Can we meet?"

I met the recruiter, a guy by the name of Gus, who was wearing tight blue jeans, big buckle, boots, and a cowboy hat. I thought, *Wow if you're going to do criminal work, this is what it's all about.* I was extremely impressed with the DEA agents and the recruiter, how they dressed, and how they acted. Gus and I later became good friends.

I got a job as a correctional officer with the Federal Bureau of Prisons. Then with Immigration & Naturalization Service (INS) reviewing documents. About a year later, I got a call from Gus, offering me a job. I was very excited to be able to work with Gus. *What a blessing to work with DEA!* I went to the DEA academy for three months in Quantico, VA. There, I had a lot of training in firearms, self-defense, tactical driving, and understanding the legal side of due process.

Randy Torgerson

Randy Torgerson served in the United States Army and worked in law enforcement before becoming a private investigator with Pearce Corporation. He continues to work as a self-employed private investigator.

The Early Years

I grew up in a small farming town in Lake Crystal, Minnesota. I started driving a 1967 Ford Galaxy 500 two-door fastback to school when I was 15. At that time, farmers' children could get a special driver's license that allowed them to drive on the highways at age 15 within 20 miles of home for farm purposes.

I kept a bag of chicken feed in my trunk in case I got pulled over by the police. I had a police scanner in my car so that I could hear the local small-town police radios.

I was driving to school one morning and could hear on the radio one cop asking another, "Is Torgerson old enough to drive?"

The other cop responded, "I guess so since he's been driving to school every day."

Little did they know, I wasn't 16 yet and driving to school was not a farm purpose.

Listening to the small-town cops talking on the scanner got me interested in law enforcement. Over the next few years, I thought about becoming a cop.

My high school graduating class in 1982 was only 52 students. After graduation, I learned I wasn't old enough to get into law enforcement, so I joined the army and went to training at Fort Benning, Georgia. After graduating in December 1983 with a Military Occupational Specialty, Infantry (MOS 11B), I spent the next four years in Germany under the United States European Command. I did security and some investigations for the Pershing II strategic nuclear missile program. I worked mainly at night patrolling around the missiles fenced locations, walking through the famous Black Forest that surrounded the site.

For me, the fun part was patrolling the Black Forest area where protesters hired by the Russians came to cause problems. The Black Forest lives up to its name. As night came, it was so dark, with no light from the moon or stars getting through the trees. Without light, it was easy to surveil the protesters. You could walk just a few feet behind them, and they wouldn't know you were there. I had state-of-the-art night-vision goggles and could move around with ease.

I got married in Germany to a German national, and we moved to Kansas. We had our son after moving back to the states. My last months in the army were at Fort Riley, Kansas. At this time, I got into law enforcement. At first, I worked part-time as a paid reserve police officer while still in the military. Then I worked undercover for a local county sheriff's office, buying dope. It turned into a full-time uniformed officer position.

After a couple of years, my marriage became stressful because I was gone so much with work. Eventually, my wife and I got divorced. I worked for about a year in Kansas City as a private investigator and then resigned when my new girlfriend and I moved out to California.

In 1992 I went to work for the Pearce Corporation with Jerry Pearce with John Crenshaw, and Jeff. Both Jeff and John were in trouble with Jerry that first week I was in the office. When they met me, they thought I was hired to replace either or both. I was hired as additional support and sent off for the first 60 days working on other cases. I later became involved for four-and-a-half years investigating the case that eventually led to the Meraz organization.

By this time, I was about 29, average height, stocky, and very personable. I played an important role, working primarily in the Los Angeles area doing a lot of the background research. I was very knowledgeable and detail-oriented about that part of the case. Jerry described me as a hard worker and up for any task that came my way. Since both Jeff and I came from a military background, we were hard workers with a shared drive to complete the mission, which was more important than anything else. Sometimes it seemed more important than family. Which later caused problems.

Eventually, my girlfriend Stephanie and I got married. We had two children, a boy, and a girl. I traveled so much for work that I was gone more than I was home, and our marriage suffered. We divorced but have remained good friends and are both supportive of our children.

Erik Hansen, another Pearce investigator, was even younger than Jeff and me. He often worked with Jeff in Yuma. And sometimes when he was needed in Los Angeles. John was also young and worked closely with me in Los Angeles and back in the office in Fresno, gathering more information on whatever case we were working.

Jeff and John worked on many cases together before this one. They were like two peas in a pod. John was very friendly, personable, enthusiastic, and a good friend to Jeff and later to me as well.

Jeffrey Pearce

Jeffrey Pearce served in the United States Army and worked as a private investigator for Pearce Corporation. He continues to work as a self-employed private investigator. Jeff Passed away in 2020.

The Early Years

When the case began, I was about 23, lean, and ready to take on the world. I ran five miles every night and considered myself to be a machine. Others told me I was a charmer with the ladies. They also called me "Big Ears," but I've grown out of that after twenty years.

I grew up in Central Valley, Fresno, California, and graduated from a vocational high school in 1987, where I focused on military and police science. While I was in high school, my Uncle Jerry offered me an internship in his company to fulfill my requirement for police science. I looked up to him and wanted to do well.

I remember Uncle Jerry once sending me to the Fresno County Public Library to look for articles about a case involving a baseball team and drugs. He wanted me to pull together all the news articles I could find related to the case. I used all the change I had to make copies of several news stories. It must have been close to 100 pages. I put everything in a manila folder.

When I walked into Uncle Jerry's office, he was sitting at his desk, smoking a cigarette. He always smoked Tarrington 100s. I handed him the folder, he opened it, flipped through a few pages, then threw them all at me. Papers were strewn all over the office.

He said, "What is this?"

I was taken aback and just looked at him.

He said, "The problem with this is it's not in date order. An assignment should look professional. It should be typed, with a summary of the story you're providing me, so I don't have to go through and read them all."

He wanted things done correctly and to the best of my ability, no matter what the job.

I had always been drawn to law enforcement. I felt it was my calling, so I enlisted in the Army right after graduation and went to Fort Jackson, South Carolina, for basic training. The military offered me the opportunity to attend college while I was stationed in New Jersey.

While training at my post at Fort Jackson, I saw a group of young ladies in a platoon marching by where we were standing. One of them caught my eye. She was a beautiful girl, and I wanted to get to know her. We started writing back and forth and after several months decided to get married.

In December 1987, I went home on leave for Christmas and married my first wife. I was sent to a communications base at Fort Gordon in Augusta, Georgia. I was in training as a communications security officer. My wife was sent to Fort Monmouth, New Jersey.

Augusta, Georgia, was a dry town. Every Friday a group of us would go out and buy several cases of beer. We put the beer in a bathtub of ice for the weekend in a room we rented at the Master's Hotel. There was a comradery of both men and women, and we partied all weekend.

We decided to apply for the married couple's program so we could live together. My first assignment was supposed to be in Manheim, Germany. The army agreed. So, I went to New Jersey to surprise her with the news that I wouldn't be going to Germany after all.

If we wanted to live together, we had to go off-base to Eaton Town, New Jersey. We were both privates, poor, and on a strict budget. We found a small one-bedroom apartment. Most of our meals were ground beef and macaroni.

We both worked hard toward getting promoted. After a few months, I was offered a position doing communications security underground at Community Electronics Command CECOM in New Jersey. I was working in a vault two floors below ground for a while. The Criminal Investigations Division (CID) approached me to do background investigations of civilian employees who wanted to work for the government and investigate stolen equipment cases. I did joint testing with civilian personnel. This job was my first taste of working with law enforcement. They made me the North Atlantic Treaty Organization (NATO) sub-control point officer. I was sent to Panama for about 45 days to do interrogations and whatever else was needed.

I was able to take military leave for two weeks to see my grandfather when he found out he had colon cancer. Uncle Jerry knew I didn't have much time left in the service, and when I saw him at Grandpa's, I told him I wanted to get into law enforcement.

He told me, "Don't get involved with the bureaucracy of law enforcement. Why don't you come work for me? I'll be sure to take care of you."

Before my grandfather died, he told me, "Son, do me one favor."

"What's that, Grandpa?"

"Do not go to work with your uncle. He's a good man, but it would be a bad decision on your part." I didn't think much of it at the time, and I never got more information from him, but I always remembered what he said.

My wife and I were still in the army when the first Gulf War began. There was a stop-loss program implemented that didn't allow anyone to get out. I was just about to get out when I was assigned to a combat military police unit with the Army Reserves in New Jersey. My wife was still in the regular army. I flew back to California to start working for Uncle Jerry. It was going to be a while before my wife would get out. I decided to fly back to New Jersey for visits until her discharge. While I was there, she got pregnant. The military provided a discharge because of her pregnancy. We drove across the country and back to California to work for Uncle Jerry.

I was young and naïve. Some of my first cases were minor, such as divorce cases where we went through bank records and receipts. We had a big case coming up and went to Santa Rosa, looking for stolen construction equipment. This case was the first time I saw my uncle in full action. He was a master at interviewing people. He was laid back and didn't press people too hard. He let others do the talking while he had a big cassette recorder going with a mic and I would take notes. He taught me a lot about dealing with informants and others involved in doing things for us as we worked our cases. I ended up working with him over the next seven years and gained a lot of experience in dealing with people.

Dianne DeMille PhD, Larry Hardin, Jeffrey Pearce, Randy Torgerson

What has happened to …?

Who?	1990s	Now?
Aduana, Peter	US Customs	
Bonner, Robert	DEA Adm, Attorney w/Grovers	Counsel for Gibson, Dunn & Crutcher in Washington D.C
Camarena, Kiki	DEA murdered/ Tortured to Death and his informant in Mexico	Deceased
Crowe, Michael	DPS (Department of Public Safety of AZ) Sgt for the Southwest Narcotic Task Force	Deceased/Assassinated by a corrupt Yuma Deputy Sheriff Officer
Diaz, Tom	San Luis, AZ Police Officer	Retired
Ehrhart, James	Retired DPS officer	Retired
Elkins, Danny	Lieutenant Yuma PD assigned to the Southwest Narcotic Task Force	Deceased/Assassinated by a corrupt Yuma Deputy Sheriff Officer
Enano	DEA CI (Confidential Informant)	Assassinated by the Mexican Cartel
Garza, Gabriel	Chief San Luis PD	Retired
Hutchinson, Jack	Yuma Deputy Sheriff Officer assigned to Southwest Narcotic Task Force	Life in AZ Prison for assassinating LT Elkins and Sgt. Crowe

Who?	1990s	Now?
Jonas Rodriguez, Jose	Meraz's right hand man	Retired
Little, Sam	DEA Agent	Retired/Last location Hong Kong
Meraz Gutierrez, Olegario	Oldest brother	Living in San Luis, Mexico. Operating a farm.
Meraz Gutierrez, Oscar	Youngest brother	Unknown living or dead in Mexico.
Meraz Gutierrez, Oswaldo	Second brother	Living in San Luis, Mexico. Operating a farm.
Norman	DEA	Retired/Contract work in Mexico
Pedro	DEA CI (Confidential Informant)	Disappeared in Mexico
Quintero, Raphael	Head of a gatekeeper in Calexico, AZ	In Mexico prison.
Salazar, Hugo	CIA operative working at Blue Finn	Unknown
Seal, Barry	Pilot transported weapons & drugs	Assassinated by the Colombian Cartel
Shorb, Ray	LAPD Major Crimes	Retired

Who?	1990s	Now?
Spencer, Mark	FBI Agent	Possible: retired FBI and returned to Mexico.
Stevenson, Roy	DEA Agent	Medical Retired from DEA/unknown location
Vasquez Mendoza, Augusto	Most wanted for assassinating a DEA Agent	Serving Life in AZ. State Prison for killing a DEA agent.
Ware, Don	DEA Agent	Medical Retired DEA agent/later died doing surgery.
Webb, Gary	Reporter	Suicide

Pearce Corporation

Who?	1990s	Now?
John	Private Investigator	In Law Enforcement
Pearce, Jeff	Private Investigator	Deceased
Pearce, Jerry		Deceased
Torgeson, Randy	Private Investigator	PI

US Attorney, Phoenix

Who?	1990s	Now?
Lost, Jimmie	AUSA	Unknown
Hope, Michael	AUSA	Possibly within the CIA world
Napoletano, Janet	US Attorney General	Faculty at Goldman School of Public Policy, elected to American Philosophical Society 2018

References

"List of Politicians killed in the Mexican drug war." *Wickepedia*. Accessed June 2017. https://www.revolvy.com/topic/List%20of%20politicians%20killed%20in%20the%20Mexican%20Drug%20War.

"Media gagged from reporting drug test results of murder suspect." *Reporters Committee for Freedom of the Press: Feature*. September 25, 1995. Accessed April 23, 2018. https://www.rcfp.org/browse-media-law-resources/news/media-gagged-reporting-drug-test-results-murder-suspect.

"Sheriffs of Yuma County." *Yuma County Sheriff's Office*. Accessed August 12, 2017. http://www.yumacountysheriff.org/about-sheriffs.html.

AFP. "Longest' drug tunnel found on California-Mexico border." *Breitbart News Network*. April 2016. http://www.breitbart.com/news/longest-drug-tunnel-found-on-california-mexico-border/.

Associated Press. "Arizona Deputy Charged With Killing Two Fellow Lawmen 'Exemplary' Narcotics Fighter Stealing Guns, Drugs From Evidence Room." July 8, 1995. Accessed April 23, 2018. http://www.spokesman.com/stories/1995/jul/08/arizona-deputy-charged-with-killing-two-fellow/.

Associated Press. "Agents Find Drug Tunnel to U.S. *The New York Times*. May 19, 1990. http://www.nytimes.com/1990/05/19/us/agents-find-drug-tunnel-to-us.html.

Attwood, Shaun. American Made: Who Killed Barry Seal? Pablo Escobar or George Bush (War on Drugs Book 2).

Bowden, Charles and Molloy, Molly. "Blood on The Corn: Into the killing room: Murder of a DEA agent, Final Installment." *Tucson Sentinel*. Posted April 7, 2015. http://www.tucsonsentinel.com/nationworld/report/040715_blood_on_the_corn3/into-killing-room-murder-dea-agent/.

Campbell, Duncan and Tuckman, Jo. "Mexicans hand over drug-tunnel smuggler." *The Guardian: World News*. June 13, 2001. https://www.theguardian.com/world/2001 /jun/14/Mexico.

Crock, Richard. "Wall of Honor, Don Ware." *Survivor's Benefit Fund*. Accessed June 12, 2017. https://www.survivorsbenefitfund.org/?fuseaction=woh.sh ow&key=ff08ca7d-a7fc-4722-b03c-77c517981b71.

De Wilde, B. "Hector Berrellez: Biography." IMDb. Accessed October 21, 2017. http://www.imdb.com/name/nm3171195/bio?ref_=nm_ov _bio_sm.

Department of Justice. "Organized Crime Drug Enforcement Task Forces." *The United States Department of Justice: Criminal Division*. Updated June 9, 2015. https://www.justice.gov/criminal/organized-crime-drug-enforcement-task-forces.

Dowbenko, Uri. "Book Review: Dark Alliance: The CIA, the Contras, and the Crack Cocaine Explosion." Conspiracy Digest: Real News That Connects the Dots ..., 2001. Accessed April 23, 2018. http://www.conspiracydigest.com/bookdark.html.

Dreamer, Richard. "Letter written to Larry Hardin." May 4, 1994. U.S. Department of Justice, U.S. States Attorney, District of Arizona.

Ferranti, Seth. "The Story Behind an Infamous Escobar Cartel Assassination." *Vice: Stuff*. March 27, 2016. https://www.vice.com/en_us/article/4w3mvw/an-fbi-agent-tells-story-behind-an-infamous-escobar-cartel-assassination.

Gallegher, Mike. "King of The Kingpins: The Mexican Federation." *Albuquerque Journal*. March 1997. https://www.abqjournal.com/news/drugs/8drug3-3.htm.

Gibson, Dunn, and Crutcher Law Firm. Accessed on June 8, 2017. http://www.gibsondunn.com.

Golden, Tim. "Cardinal in Mexico Killed in a Shooting Tied to Drug Battle" *New York Times*. May 25, 1993.

http://www.nytimes.com/1993/05/25/world/cardinal-in-mexico-killed-in-a-shooting-tied-to-drug-battle.html.

Grant, Will. "Mexico drugs: How one DEA killing began a brutal war. BBC News, Guadalajara." February 2012. http://www.bbc.com/news/world-us-canada-16920870.

ISGP. "Kiki Camarena's Murder and Torture Described: CIA's Felix Rodriguez and Mexican Government Officials Involved in DEA Agent's Death." *Globalization and Covert Politics*. ISGP sections: Suspicious deaths index: Four dozen CIA drug trafficking cases. Accessed June 27, 2017. https://isgpstudies.com/DL_1985_DEA_agent_torture_with_Mexican_ officials_present.

Kraul, Chris. "From torture to terrorism: How DEA case let to extraordinary rendition." *Los Angeles Times*. February 26, 2015. http://www.latimes.com/world/mexico-americas/la-fg-dea-camarena-20150226-story.html.

Levine, Michael. "Phone Call with DEA Agent Michael Levine about 'Kiki' Camarena drugs and the CIA Corruption." Accessed May 5, 2018. https://www.youtube.com/watch?v=2nFY3wiGIQE.

Lisalus, Som. "Drug Tunnel Architect Faces 20 years." *Tuscon News Now: KOLD New 13*. Accessed August 9, 2017. http://www.tucsonnewsnow.com/story/4710820/drug-tunnel-architect-faces-20-years.

Merentes, Luis A. "Was the CIA behind 'Kiki' Camerena's Murder? Investigative Journalist and Congress Must Follow Up." Huffington Post. December 15, 2013. Accessed September 29, 2017.

Milford, Rob. "Mexican Authorities Discover Massive Smuggling Tunnel Before Completion." *Breitbart*. April 2015. http://www.breitbart.com/texas/2015/04/08/mexican-authorities-discover-massive-smuggling-tunnel-before-completion/

Mora, Edwin. "DEA: 224 Mexican Cartel Border Tunnels Found Since 1990." *Breitbart*. Dec 13, 2016.

http://www.breitbart.com/texas/2016/12/13/dea-224-mexican-cartel-tunnels-found-since-1990/.

Mora, Edwin. "DHS IG: Tunnels Along U.S. – Mexico Border 'Significant and Growing' Threat." *Breitbart*. Dec. 13, 2013. http://www.breitbart.com/big-government/2013/12/13/dhs-ig-tunnels-along-us-mexico%20border-significant-and-growing-threat/.

Morrison, Jane Ann. "Shooting didn't end DEA agent's love for job and desire to live." *Las Vegas Review Journal*. May 14, 2011. http://www.pressreader.com/usa/las-vegas-review-journal/20110514/281831460312733.

Multiple Authors. "Narcotics agent held in deaths of 2 Yuma officers." *Tucson Citizen*: *Local*. July 6, 1995. http://tucsoncitizen.com/morgue2/1995/07/06/99618-narcotics-agent-held-in-deaths-of-2-yuma-officers/.

Murillo, Lupita. "Crime Trackers: El Chapo's first tunnel was built in Southern Arizona 25 years ago." News 4 Tucson. July 14, 2015. http://www.kvoa.com/story/29549256/crime-trackers-el-chapos-first-tunnel-was-built-in-southern-arizona-25-years-ago.

Murphy, Kim. "Agent, 2 Drug Suspects Killed in Gun Battles: 2nd DEA Man Is Brain Dead as Shoot-Out, Auto Chase Stun Posh Pasadena, San Marino Areas." *Los Angeles Times*. February 6, 1988. http://articles.latimes.com/1988-02-06/news/mn-10492_1_san-marino.

Murphy, Kim. "2 Suspected Dealers Charged in Murder of DEA Agents." *Los Angeles Times*. March 15, 1988. http://articles.latimes.com/1988-03-15/local/me-1075_1_dea-agent.

Mydans, Seth. "Agents Seize 20 Tons of Cocaine In Raid on Los Angeles Warehouse." The New York Times. September 30, 1989. http://www.nytimes.com/1989-09-30/us/agents-seize-20-tons-of-cocaine-in-raid-on-los-angeles-warehouse.html?pagewanted=print.

Newton, Jim. "Camerena's Abduction and Torture Described: Courts." *Los Angeles Times*. December 10, 1992.

http://articles.latimes.com/1992-12-10/local/me-
2364_1_ranking-mexican.

NPR. "The Forgotten War on Drugs – Timeline: America's War
on Drugs." National Public Radio (NPR), based on
reporting from PBS' Frontline Series. Accessed on July 5,
2017.
http://www.npr.org/templates/story/php?/storyId=9252490

NSC. "The Contras, Cocaine, and Covert Operations." *The
National Security Archive Electronic Briefing Book No. 2.*
NSC Declassified Documents. Accessed July 17, 2017.
http://nsarchive.gwu.edu/NSAEBB/NSAEBB2/index.html
#1.

Parker, Richard. "Mexico's Poor Trading Machetes for AK-47s."
Journal Washington Bureau: A Journal Special Report.
March 1997. https://www.abqjournal.com/news/drugs/.

Reel, Monty. "How El Chapo Builds His Tunnels. *The New
Yorker*. August 3, 2013.
http://www.newyorker.com/magazine/2015/08/03/underw
orld-monte-reel.

Ross, Brian. *NBC News*. February 20, 1986. Published on
Youtube, August 30, 2012.

Rush, Tim. "The PAN Party of Drug Trafficking, organized
crime, and dirty money." *Executive Intelligence Review*.
12, no. 23, June 10, 1985. 29-30.
http://www.larouchepub.com/eiw/public/1985/eirv12n23-
19850610/eirv12n23-19850610_029-
the_pan_party_of_drug_traffickin.pdf.

Schou, Nick. "The truth in 'Dark Alliance.'" Los Angeles Times.
August 18, 2006. Accessed on June 27, 2017.
http://articles.latimes.com/2006/aug/18/opinion/oe-
schou18

Sheridan, Mary Beth. Mexico Arrests Suspect in Killing of DEA
Agent. Los Angeles Times. July 11, 2000.
http://articles.latimes.com /2000/jul/11/news/mn-51073.
The Associated Press. Slain agent's family files a $6
million suit against DEA. *Tucson Citizen*. August 19,
1996.

Simon, Dan. "The Tragedy of Gary Webb." *The Progressive*. June 27, 2013. Accessed May 7, 2015. https://progressive.org/dispatches/tragedy-gary-webb/.

Soble, Ronald L. "6 Go on Trial in Record Drug Bust in Sylmar." Los Angeles Times. September 20, 1990. Accessed July 5. 2017. http://articles.latimes.com/1990-09-20/local/me-885_1_drug-seizure.

St. Clair, Jeffrey. "Air Cocaine: The Wild, True Story of Drug-Running, Arms Smuggling and Contras at a Backwoods Airstrip in the Clintons' Arkansas." *CounterPunch*, November 2016. https://www.counterpunch.org/2016/11/04/air-cocaine-the-wild-true-story-of-drug-running-arms-smuggling-and-contras-at-a-small-airstrip-in-clintons-arkansas/.

Stewart, Bob W. "United States May Ask State to Prosecute in DEA Ambush." *Los Angeles Times.* February 25, 1988. Accessed May 5, 2018. https://www.newspapers.com/newspage/404160312/.

Storrs, K. Larry. "Mexico Misc. FOIA." *CRS Report for Congress*. March 30, 2001. https://archive.org/stream/MexicoFOIA/Mexico's%20Counter-Narcotics%20Efforts%20under%20Zedillo%20and%20Fox,%20December%201994-March%202001_djvu.txt.

Sutton, Candace, NewsComAu, April 17, 2013. *Herald Sun.* Accessed May 17, 2018. http://www.heraldsun.com.au/news/world/the-waco-massacre-a-fiery-end-to-a-whacko-cult/news story/6b20c291b99ecab63c0ab7816c79d830?sv=a03620418dc9b82bd1cf7e4810edcda4.

Taubman, Philip. "Worry Over Illegal Arms Exports Growing Among Prosecutors." New York Times: Archives, 1981. Accessed May 22, 2018. https://www.nytimes.com/1981/07/ 14/us/worry-over-illegal-arms-exports-growing-among-us-prosecutors.html.

United Press International: UPI Archives. July 14, 1995. "Police say evidence theft led to killings.

http://www.upi.com/Archives/1995/07/14/Police-say-evidece-theft-led-to-killings/8785805694400/.

United States Court of Appeals, Ninth Circuit. "Michael Su CHIA, Petitioner-Appellant, v. Steven CAMBRA, Jr., Warden; Attorney General of the State of California, Respondents-Appellees. No. 99-56361." March 4, 2004. Accessed May 5, 2018. https://caselaw. findlaw.com/us-9th-circuit/1241789.html.

Vazquez, Juan M. "Mexico: U.S. Bitter." *Los Angeles Times*, March 17, 1985, 31. https://latimes.newspapers.com/image/172726453/?terms=camarena.

Webb, Gary. "Dark Alliance: Gary Webb's Incendiary 1996 SJ Mercury News Exposé." Downloaded from *Seattle Times*, Daniel Pouzzner, Ed. Accessed June 27, 2017. http://www.mega.nu/ampp/webb.html.

Webb, Gary. 1998. *Dark Alliance: The CIA, the Contras, and The Crack Cocaine Explosion.* About Dark Alliance. Author's Notes. Seven Stories Press: New York.

Wiedrich, Bob. "Acts of Heroism in Narcotics War." *Chicago Tribune*. June 18, 1975, page 28. http://archives.chicagotribune.com/1975/06/18/page/28/article/acts-of-heroism-in-narcotics-war.

Williams, Montel. "Kill the Messenger; Mike Levine & Gary Webb – The Big White Lie + Dark Alliance= CIA drug cartel. Accessed May 5, 2018. https://www.youtube.com/watch?v=LG8XNFPBPUs.

Ybarra, Michael J. and Ford, Andrea. "Jury Finds Man Guilty in Murder of 2 DEA Agents." *Los Angeles Times*. November 2, 1988. http://articles.latimes.com/1988-11-02/local/me-573_1_three-dea-agents.

Dianne DeMille PhD, Larry Hardin, Jeffrey Pearce, Randy Torgerson

Notes

---

1 Mike Gallegher. "King of The Kingpins: The Mexican Federation." Albuquerque Journal. March 1997, Day 2. https://www.abqjournal.com /news/drugs/8drug3-3.htm.

[2] Ibid.

[3] Tim Rush. "The PAN Party of Drug Trafficking, organized crime, and dirty money." *Executive Intelligence Review*. 12, no. 23, June 10, 1985. 30. http://www.larouchepub.com/eiw/public/1985/eirv12n23-19850610/eirv12n23-19850610_029-the_pan_party_of_drug_traffickin.pdf.

[4] Rush.

[5] Interview with Larry Hardin.

[6] Juan M. Vazquez. "Mexico: U.S. Bitter." *Los Angeles Times*, March 17, 1985, 31. https://latimes.newspapers.com/image/172726453/?terms=camarena

[7] Chris Kraul. "From torture to terrorism: How DEA case let to extraordinary rendition." Los Angeles Times. February 26, 2015. http://www.latimes.com/world/mexico-americas/la-fg-dea-camarena-20150226-story.html.

[8] Vasquez.

[9] Ibid.

[10] Ibid.

[11] Kraul.

[12] B. De Wilde. "Hector Berrellez: Biography." IMDb. Accessed October 21, 2017. http://www.imdb.com/name/nm3171195/bio? Ref

[13] Will Grant. "Mexico drugs: How one DEA killing began a brutal war." BBC News, Guadalajara. February 2012. http://www.bbc.com/news/ world-us-canada-16920870

[14] James Newton. "Camerena's Abduction and Torture Described: Courts." Los Angeles Times. December 10, 1992. http://articles. latimes.com/1992-12-10/local/me-2364_1_ranking-mexican.

[15] Hardin.

[16] Luis A. Merentes. "Was the CIA behind 'Kiki' Camerena's Murder? Investigative Journalist and Congress Must Follow Up." *The HuffPost: The Blog*. December 15, 2013, Accessed September 29, 2017.

[17] Kraul.

[18] Ibid.

[19] Merentes.

[20] Hardin.

[21] Hardin.

[22] DoJ. "Organized Crime Drug Enforcement Task Forces." *The United States Department of Justice: Criminal Division.* Updated, June 9, 2015. Accessed August 14, 2017. https://www.justice.gov/criminal/ organized-crime-drug-enforcement-task-forces.

[23] Ibid.

[24] Edwin Mora. "DHS IG: Tunnels Along United States – Mexico Border 'Significant and Growing' Threat." *Breitbart.* Dec. 13, 2013. http://www.breitbart.com/big-government/2013/12/13/dhs-ig-tunnels-along-us-mexico%20border-significant-and-growing-threat/.

[25] Ibid.

[26] Som Lisalus. “Drug Tunnel Architect Faces 20 years.” *Tucson News Now: KOLD New 13*. Accessed August 9, 2017. http://www.tucsonnewsnow.com/story/4710820/drug-tunnel-architect-faces-20-years.

[27] Associated Press. "Agents Find Drug Tunnel to the United States *The New York Times*. May 19, 1990. http://www.nytimes.com/1990/05/19/us/agents-find-drug-tunnel-to-us.html.

[28] Monty Reel. “How El Chapo Builds His Tunnels. *The New Yorker*. August 3, 2013. http://www.newyorker.com/magazine/2015/08/03/ underworld-monte-reel.

[29]Campbell, Duncan, and Tuckman, Jo. "Mexicans hand over drug-tunnel smuggler." *The Guardian: World News*. June 13, 2001. https://www.theguardian.com/world/2001/jun/14/mexico

[30] Richard Parker. “Mexico’s Poor Trading Machetes for AK-47s.” *Journal Washington Bureau: A Journal Special Report*. March 1997. https://www.abqjournal.com/news/drugs.

[31] Mora.

[32] Ibid.

[33] Seth Mydans. “Agents Seize 20 Tons of Cocaine In Raid on Los Angeles Warehouse.” The New York Times. September 30, 1989. http://www.nytimes.com/1989-09-30/us/agents-seize-20-tons-of-cocaine-in-raid-on-los-angeles-warehouse.html?pagewanted=print.

[34] Soble, Ronald L. “6 Go on Trial in Record Drug Bust in Sylmar.” Los Angeles Times. September 20, 1990. Http://articles.latimes .com/1990-09-20/local/me-885_1_drug-seizure.

[35] Tim Golden. “Cardinal in Mexico Killed in a Shooting Tied to Drug Battle” *New York Times.* May 25, 1993.

http://www.nytimes.com/1993/05/25/world/cardinal-in-mexico-killed-in-a-shooting-tied-to-drug-battle.html

36 Hardin.

37 Ibid.

38 Ibid.

39 Gibson, Dunn, and Crutcher Law Firm. Accessed on June 8, 2017. http://www.gibsondunn.com.

40 Jeffrey St. Clair. "Air Cocaine: The Wild, True Story of Drug-Running, Arms Smuggling and Contras at a Backwoods Airstrip in the Clintons' Arkansas." *CounterPunch*, November 2016. https://www.counterpunch.org/2016/11/04/air-cocaine-the-wild-true-story-of-drug-running-arms-smuggling-and-contras-at-a-small-airstrip-in-clintons-arkansas/.

41 Ibid.

42 Ibid.

43 Ibid.

44 Seth Ferranti. "The Story Behind an Infamous Escobar Cartel Assassination." Vice: Stuff. Accessed June 20, 2017. https://www.vice.com/en_us/article/4w3mvw/an-fbi-agent-tells-story-behind-an-infamous-escobar-cartel-assassination.

45 NPR. "The Forgotten War on Drugs – Timeline: America's War on Drugs." National Public Radio (NPR), based on reporting from PBS' Frontline Series, 17. Accessed on July 5, 2017. http://www.npr.org/templates/story/php?/storyId=9252490.

46 NSC. "The Contras, Cocaine, and Covert Operations." The National Security Archive Electronic Briefing Book No. 2. NSC Declassified Documents. Accessed July 17, 2017. http://nsarchive. gwu.edu/NSAEBB/NSAEBB2/index.html#1.

47 Shaun Attwood. American Made: Who Killed Barry Seal? Pablo Escobar or George HW Bush: War on Drugs.

[48] Ibid.

[49] St. Clair.

[50] Ibid.

[51] Ibid.

[52] Attwood, 1.

[53] Ibid.

[54] Ibid.

[55] Ferranti, 1.

[56] Interview with Randy Torgerson.

[57] Hardin.

[58] Ibid.

[59] St. Clair.

[60] "Huang Visited White House 65 Times This Year." Deseret News. October 31, 1996. http://www.deseretnews.com/article/522473/HUANG-VISITED-WHITE-HOUSE-65-TIMES-THIS-YEAR.html

[61] Anne Farris. "Unfolding Story Swelling Like a Sponge." Washington Post: Politics Campaign Finance Special Report. April 6, 1997, A16. http://www.washingtonpost.com/wp-srv/politics/special/campfin/stories/story.htm

[62] Michael J. Ybarra and Andrea Ford. "Jury Finds Man Guilty in Murder of 2 DEA Agents. Los Angeles Times. November 2, 1988.

[63] United States Court of Appeals, Ninth Circuit. "Michael Su CHIA, Petitioner-Appellant, v. Steven CAMBRA, Jr., Warden; Attorney General of the State of California, Respondents-Appellees. No. 99-56361." March 4, 2004. Accessed May 5, 2018. https://caselaw. findlaw.com/us-9th-circuit/1241789.html.

[64] Ibid.

[65] Bob W. Stewart. "United States May Ask State to Prosecute in DEA Ambush." Los Angeles Times. February 25, 1988.

[66] Ybarra and Ford

[67] Gary Webb. "Dark Alliance: Gary Webb's Incendiary 1996 SJ Mercury News Exposé." Downloaded from Seattle Times, Daniel Pouzzner, Ed. Accessed June 27, 2017. http://www.mega.nu/ampp/webb.html.

[68] Torgeson

[69] Ibid.

[70] Ibid.

[71] Gary Webb. 1998. *Dark Alliance: The CIA, the Contras, and The Crack Cocaine Explosion.* About Dark Alliance. Author's Notes. Seven Stories Press: New York.

[72] Ibid, 2.

[73] Ibid, 2.

[74] Montel Williams. "Kill the Messenger; Mike Levine & Gary Webb – The Big White Lie + Dark Alliance= CIA drug cartel. Accessed May 5, 2018. https://www.youtube.com/watch?v=LG8XNFPBPUs.

[75] Nick Schou. "The truth in 'Dark Alliance.'" Los Angeles Times. August 18, 2006.

[76] Gary Webb. "Kill the Messenger: Plot Summary." IMDb.

[77] Dan Simon "The Tragedy of Gary Webb." *The Progressive.* June 27, 2013. Accessed May 7, 2015. https://progressive.org/dispatches/tragedy-gary-webb/.

[78] Ibid.

[79] Schou.

[80] Gary Webb "Inside the Dark Alliance: Gary Webb on the CIA, the Contras, and the Crack Cocaine Explosion." Democracy Now, October 6, 2014, 2.

[81] Uri Dowbenko. "Book Review: Dark Alliance: The CIA, the Contras, and the Crack Cocaine Explosion." Conspiracy Digest: Real News That Connects the Dots ..., 2001.

[82] Michael Levine. "Phone Call with DEA Agent Michael Levine about 'Kiki' Camarena drugs and the CIA Corruption." Accessed May 5, 2018. https://www.youtube.com/watch?v=2nFY3wiGIQE.

[83] Ibid.

[84] Hardin.

[85] Mary Beth Sheridan. Mexico Arrests Suspect in Killing of DEA Agent. Los Angeles Times. July 11, 2000. http://articles.latimes.com /2000/jul/11/news/mn-51073. The Associated Press. Slain agent's family files a $6 million suit against DEA. *Tucson Citizen*. August 19, 1996.

[86] Ibid.

[87] Hardin

[88] Sheridan.

[89] Richard Dreamer. "Letter written to Larry Hardin." May 4, 1994. United States Department of Justice, United States States Attorney, District of Arizona.

[90] ISGP. "Kiki Camarena's Murder and Torture Described: CIA's Felix Rodriguez and Mexican Government Officials Involved in DEA Agent's Death." Globalization and Covert Politics. ISGP sections: Suspicious deaths index: Four dozen CIA drug trafficking cases. Accessed June 27, 2017. https://isgpstudies.com/DL_1985_DEA_agent_torture_with_Mexican_officials_present.

[91] United Press International. "Police say evidence theft led to killings." United Press International: UPI Archives. July 14, 1995. http://www.upi.com/Archives/1995/07/14/Police-say-evidece-theft-led-to-killings/8785805694400/.

[92] Associated Press. "Arizona Deputy Charged With Killing Two Fellow Lawmen 'Exemplary' Narcotics Fighter Stealing Guns, Drugs From Evidence Room." July 8, 1995. April 23, 2018. http://www.spokesman.com/stories/1995/jul/08/arizona-deputy-charged-with-killing-two-fellow/.

[93] Ibid.

[94] Hardin

[95] Multiple Authors. "Narcotics agent held in deaths of 2 Yuma officers." *Tucson Citizen*: *Local*. July 6, 1995.

[96] UPI. "Police say evidence theft led to killings." *UPI Archives*. July 14, 1995.

[97] "Media gagged from reporting drug test results of murder suspect." *Reporters Committee for Freedom of the Press: Feature*. September 25, 1995.

[98] Associated Press. "Arizona Deputy Charged With Killing Two Fellow Lawmen 'Exemplary' Narcotics Fighter Stealing Guns, Drugs From Evidence Room." *The Spokesman-Review: Nation/World*. July 8, 1995.

[99] Dreamer.

[100] Pearce.

DEA PRB 10-10-18-4.